ST MARTIN'S

TRUE CRIME
CLASSICS

It wasn't much of a grave, and there wasn't much left of the body, except for the godawful smell. The experienced cop's work had brought him in close contact with long-dead bodies before, and the odor was as unforgettable as it was unmistakable. It wasn't the normal cloying putrid odor of decaying flesh that was so overpoweringly strong that it clung to clothing and skin long after the body was carted away to the morgue. The remains of the body half sticking out of the puddle of yellow and brown gravelly dirt was different. The odor it gave off was strangely sweet and metallic, and so harsh that it made the eyes burn. . . .

ST. MARTIN'S PAPERBACKS TITLES
BY CLIFFORD L. LINEDECKER

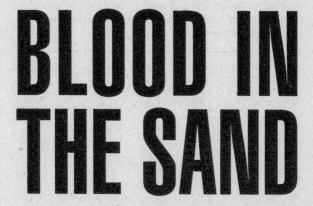

BLOOD IN THE SAND

CLIFFORD L. LINEDECKER

St. Martin's Paperbacks

BLOOD IN THE SAND

Copyright © 2000 by Clifford L. Linedecker.

Cover photograph courtesy *Las Vegas Sun*.

ISBN: 0-312-97509-0
EAN: 80312-97509-8

Printed in the United States of America

St. Martin's Paperbacks edition / August 2000

St. Martin's Paperbacks are published by St. Martin's Press, 175 Fifth Avenue, New York, NY 10010.

10 9 8 7 6 5 4 3 2

ACKNOWLEDGMENTS

The assistance and cooperation of many people contributed to the creation of this book, and they have earned my gratitude.

Among those who consented to interviews and otherwise provided assistance are officers with the Las Vegas Metro Police Department and the St. Lucie County (Florida) Sheriff's Department. My special thanks go to Case Detectives Paul Bigham and Thomas D. Thowsen in Las Vegas; and to Captain Robert Miller, Sergeant Diane M. Thompson, and Detectives Derrick Peterson and Charles Scavuzzo. Chief Deputy District Attorney David J. J. Roger in Las Vegas deserves thanks for the insights into the characters of the co-defendants in the Bruce Weinstein murder case, and into some of the more complex inner workings of the court proceedings. Roger is a prosecutor's prosecutor, and it was a pleasure meeting with him.

The hard-working, courteous staff with the Clark County Clerk's Office went out of their way to be helpful. Others who preferred to remain unnamed also contributed greatly to preparation of the final manuscript and their kind assistance is most appreciated.

Finally, my thanks go to my agent Ed Breslin of the Ed Breslin Agency in New York, to my longtime editor at St. Martin's Press, Charles Spicer, and his industrious, efficient assistant, Dorsey Mills.

AUTHOR'S NOTE

This account is totally nonfiction, and the events recounted here are true. They happened, and they are recorded as accurately and faithfully as it is within the author's ability to do. No names have been changed. Conversations and quotes are taken from the recollections of law enforcement officers and other individuals familiar with the case who were interviewed by the author, from statements in legal files, and from testimony in court proceedings. In occasional instances where accounts or recollections conflict with each other, I have either used the story that is most plausible, or presented both while citing sources, so the reader can decide for him- or herself which to believe. In a few instances, incidents are reviewed slightly out of chronological order to facilitate smoothing out the narrative and making the story more readable.

September 1999

CONTENTS

"Once In Love With Amy"

TITLE OF SONG BY FRANK LOESSER
VIRGIN MUSIC 1958

BLOOD IN
THE SAND

INTRODUCTION

To most people, Las Vegas is synonymous with gambling and glitter; a slightly, pleasingly sinful fairyland for adults where they can watch the most entertaining performers and biggest names in show business in between bouts of indulging in games of chance that everyone knows favor the house. Local business boosters call Las Vegas "Fun City" or "The Entertainment Capital of the World."

But just about everyone except the most hard-core Chamber of Commerce types knows the desert gaming mecca for lustier, grubbier pursuits that have earned it a worldwide reputation as "Sin City." Las Vegas is really about gambling, and the offshoot businesses attracted by the twenty-four-hour-a-day, 365-day-a-year preoccupation with gaming, like loan-sharking, prostitution, pawn shops, tiny little offices offering walk-in criminal defense services—even marriage chapels. Gamblers, at least nonprofessionals, tend to be impulsive people who are obsessed with chance-taking and do things on the spur of the moment.

Other cities may boast of local heroes like former Presidents, generals, baseball players, or ice-skating queens. In Las Vegas, the hall-of-famers whose names are passed around blackjack tables, roulette wheels, and keno parlors are more likely to be people like poker greats Amarillo Slim, William Walter Boyd, and Tom McEvoy, or Frank "Lefty" Rosenthal, former sports gambler, oddsmaker and host of a Strip hotel TV show who survived a Mob car-bombing. Going even further back to frontier days, the card-playing, gunslinging exploits of Old West gamblers like Poker Alice, or Wild Bill Hickok—who was shot playing poker, and died holding the now-famous "dead-man's hand": two pair, of aces and eights—are sometimes recalled.

It may be true that Las Vegas can't match the colorful ambiance of New Orleans or San Francisco, and isn't a world film center like Los Angeles, or a financial and media hub like New York. But there is no place else in America that can match its appeal for gamblers and big-time show business. The site of the city that early Spanish explorers claimed for their country and named Las Vegas, "The Meadows," is unique.

The reputation of the dusty, sun-baked settlement near the southernmost apex of the Silver State, that is sandwiched like the tip of a vulture's beak between California and Arizona, has always been a bit grubby. During the rowdy frontier days, gamblers and miners attracted by the gold and silver discovered in the nearby mountains settled their disputes with six-shooters or Bowie knives. Before that, Paiute Indians bet blankets, horses, and wives on the roll of colored bones, sticks, and stones.

Las Vegas didn't really begin coming into its own as a modern-day international tourist center and gaming mecca until a handsome, vicious hoodlum who grew up in Brooklyn and was a co-founder of Murder, Incorporated, blew into town with plans to build a grandiose gambling casino right there in the middle of the desert.

Benjamin "Bugsy" Siegel was the Mob's glamour boy, a flashy Romeo who could charm Hollywood starlets with one look from his dreamy baby-blue eyes, or dispassionately preside over the cold-blooded murder and dismemberment of one of his closest friends.

Siegel's dream of constructing the Flamingo hotel and casino, and founding a Mob-financed gambling empire in the isolated little desert town was eventually realized, but he never lived to enjoy it. Construction took far too long, and he spent so much money over projected costs that impatient Mob bosses began suspecting that he was skimming payoffs from contractors. Then the grand opening flopped, new suspicions developed that he was dipping his hand into the take, and the Mafia godfathers dispatched a pair of hitmen to end Bugsy's career and his life. A sniper crouching in the shadows outside the swank Beverly Hills home of his girlfriend, Virginia Hill, shot out one of his baby-blue eyes with a .30-.30 rifle, and blew chunks of his brain all over the living room.

Ironically, after Siegel's murder on June 20, 1947, the Flamingo made millions of dollars for the Mob, and attracted other investors who constructed a glittering parade of casinos along an entertainment corridor known all over the world as the Strip. Today the Las Vegas Strip is dotted with luxury theme hotels and gambling halls with names like the Stardust, MGM Grand, Circus-Circus, Luxor, and most recently the $1.5-billion-dollar Venetian resort-casino. International film queen Sophia Loren flew in from Italy to cut the ribbon at the grand opening of the 35-story, 3,036-room resort constructed on the former site of one of the city's pioneer casinos, the Sands. The Venetian replicates some of the most famous landmarks in Venice, and has a 586,000-gallon lagoon with working gondolas.

Since Siegel's time, Las Vegas has made many gangsters, gamblers, entertainers and cunning entrepreneurs incredibly powerful and rich. Men like Anthony "The Ant" Spilotro, a vicious Chicago Mob enforcer and model for the Joe Pesci character in the movie *Casino*; "Fat Herbie" Blitzstein, Ted Binion—and Bruce Charles Weinstein—prospered there and became men of power and high status in the particular gambling-driven milieu of Las Vegas society. Then they were murdered—or died under mysterious circumstances.

Las Vegas is not only dangerous for men, but it eats women alive. Scores of pretty young women from all over the country stream into Las Vegas every day on jetliners, Greyhound buses and driving their own cars, looking for fame and fortune. They're more likely to wind up as strippers, nude models, around-the-clock outcall prostitutes with escort services, or sticking needles into their arms than they are to land a legitimate job as a lounge singer or casino showgirl. In a recent edition of the Las Vegas Yellow Pages, listings for the sex industry took up 134 pages, and it's easier to get a Sin City hooker to make a housecall than a doctor.

The smart women, or the lucky ones, work in the casinos and clubs as croupiers, card dealers, waitresses, and bartenders, or they exist totally outside the gaming and vice business, as homemakers, secretaries, and professional women. Some are talented professionals like Amy Rica DeChant, an ambitious, imaginative, hard-driving woman who seemed to be on her way to earning—or marrying—a million dollars.

Then she met Bruce Charles Weinstein, and for both the gold digger and the gambler, the wheel of fortune took a disastrous spin.

PROLOGUE

Based on most conceptions of nudist camps, they are about the last place in the world anyone would expect to find a man or woman with something to hide. Amy DeChant was a woman with plenty of secrets to conceal, and for months she hid out in plain sight at the Sunnier Palms Resort, a popular nudist camp near Fort Pierce on South Florida's Gold Coast.

The forty-nine-year-old fugitive was a sexy, exciting woman who had a reputation as the Queen of Sunnier Palms, where she took an enthusiastic part in the recreational activities, lounging by the pool, pairing off for rousing games of volleyball, relaxing on long nature walks, soaking in hot tubs, and occasionally dancing to live music. Other residents of the resort knew the active, witty nudist as Sandy Wade.

Then *America's Most Wanted* blew her cover. On Saturday night, January 3, 1998, the popular nationally syndicated television show broadcast a program identifying Amy as "the Black Widow of Las Vegas," a fugitive suspected in the grisly murder of her boyfriend, Bruce Charles Weinstein.

The popular middle-aged woman with the acorn-brown hair, sparkling blue eyes, and the slender, tanned body of a teenager, had been on the run and hiding out off-and-on for nearly eighteen months, and as soon as she learned she was about to be profiled in the latest segment of the crime-fighting show, she packed a suitcase, slipped into a skirt and blouse, shoved her feet into a pair of practical pumps, and cleared out of the nudist camp. Within minutes of the broadcast, more than a half-dozen calls were placed to the show's telephone hotline, reporting that a woman named Sandy Wade who looked just like Amy DeChant was living with a boyfriend in his trailer at Sunnier Palms.

Amy acted just in time. She fled the nudist camp only a few hours ahead of a posse of FBI agents who showed up to place her under arrest. She was on her own, and on the run.

CHAPTER ONE

THE GAMBLER

When Sylvia White didn't get her usual morning phone call from her son, Bruce, on Saturday, July 6, 1996, she didn't like it at all. It wasn't like him not to check in, and she was still worried when she left her Summerlin-area home on the far eastern edge of Las Vegas at about 7 a.m. to drive to work.

Even though Bruce Weinstein lived only a few minutes away from his parents' house; Sylvia and Fred White could always count on his calls, because their oldest son was a creature of habit. He had a routine, and he rarely varied from it. If he went out to dinner, which he often did, he was sure to return home early, and was usually in bed by 9 or 9:30 p.m. He didn't venture away from his home late at night, because he was always up at the crack of dawn, never later than 5 or 6 a.m. Before turning in, he always telephoned his parents, just as he did a few hours later after getting out of bed to begin his morning activities. He had to arise early, because he had important work to do.

Sylvia White was closely involved with that work, and had been for a long time. She worked with her son. Running a sports book was a family business, and Bruce had taken naturally to it. He was the one everyone, family members and other employees, depended on to keep the operation running smoothly. Sylvia's concern continued to build and deepen as she left her house and drove across town on her way to work.

Shawn Hallman was puzzled. He needed an advance on his paycheck to tide him over the weekend, but he couldn't locate Bruce. Normal opening time for the betting office was 8 a.m., when the lines were set, but Hallman had come in to work at about 7:30 Saturday morning so he could call his boss.

Bruce's live-in girlfriend Amy De Chant answered the phone. She started giving him a song and dance about Bruce being upstairs in bed and sleeping late, but immediately corrected herself: "No, no. He's out," she stammered. "He'll be back around 11 a.m." That sounded strange to Hallman, but even though Bruce was his former brother-in-law and they had a close relationship, he was in no position to argue with his boss's live-in girlfriend. The young betting clerk mumbled a puzzled "Okay," and hung up. He figured he could ask for the advance after Bruce called Shawn's roommate, Brian Foster, to set the betting lines.

Foster was Bruce's office manager and line-setter, and he was mildly surprised when his boss failed to call him at 7 a.m. for their first discussion of the day about the games scheduled to be played, about the odds and setting the lines. When Bruce still hadn't called by 7:30, Foster was at a loss to figure out what was going on. It was critical to the operation to set the lines and get them on the board early, because Las Vegas is three hours behind the East Coast, and by 8 a.m. in Nevada, gamblers in New York, Boston, and other cities miles away are already beginning to call in with their bets.

The office manager was authorized to accept most bets called in to clerks manning the bank of telephones, but if a gambler called in with a bet that was unusually large, then he had to ask for Bruce's approval. Foster could make minor changes in the lines on his own, but needed Bruce's okay for everything else. Bruce was the boss and setting the lines was his call. He was the brains behind the operation and the man with the final say-so.

The two men talked during the workday at least every half-hour, often more frequently. Bruce was a man who was married to his job, and Foster had always been able to get in touch with him, regardless of where he was or who he was with. Even when Bruce was vacationing in Miami Beach, the two men had talked by phone every day. During the busiest times of those days, it was every ten minutes.

By 7:45 a.m., all the betting office employees, including Bruce's mother, had trooped into the house on Winterpine and were still waiting around staring expectantly at the telephones and at the board, as if the lines might somehow miraculously appear there. But their boss didn't call at 7:45, and by the 8 o'clock opening time he still hadn't phoned in. Normally, Bruce and his line-setter talked by phone three or four times between the first call of the morning, at 7 a.m., and 8:25, when the 800 lines were just beginning to warm up.

Foster, a boardman, four clerks, and Bruce's mother were all waiting, looking more worried and perplexed by the minute. Sylvia White sat next to Foster and helped out with whatever chores had to be taken care of. She knew the business and was an efficient, enthusiastic worker, but she couldn't set the lines. Foster had to get hold of his boss if he was going to start putting information on the board.

Then Bruce vanished. He punched in the number at Bruce's house at 8:25 a.m., desperate to get the lines set, but also motivated by the growing fear that something was disastrously wrong. After the phone rang a few times it was answered by Kenny Reisch. Reisch told Foster that he hadn't seen or heard from their boss.

Foster knew that Bruce was a man of habit, and was shaken by the brief conversation. He'd last talked with him at about 9 or 9:30 Friday night, and they had had a routine conversation. Bruce had just gotten home from the Holiday Inn where he was playing the horses, and was getting ready to go to bed. He was grumbling because the Atlanta Braves had won again, and everyone bets on the Braves. Baseball season was a bitch for bookies.

Everything about the conversation Friday night was normal, and Bruce hadn't said a word about anything special coming up on Saturday that might interfere with his usual routine, or keep him from calling in to set the lines. Foster had seen the business go through troubling times before, like when Bruce had moved the betting office from its initial location on Cedar Avenue to Winterpine after the police raid. But police raids on betting offices were expected occasionally, and bookies and their employees know how to roll with the punches.

The boss's mysterious vanishing at the beginning of a busy weekend a few days before baseball's break for the annual all-star game was a different story altogether. Nothing like this had ever happened since Foster started working for Bruce.

The office manager began dialing numbers on other lines. He tried all of Bruce's cellular phone numbers and his car phone, then finally dialed his boss's private number.

Bruce's girlfriend answered, and sounded as though the call had awakened her. She didn't bother with pleasantries, and simply advised the alarmed office manager that Bruce was gone. She agreed to leave a message for him to call the office.

Foster turned and looked at Bruce's mother. His concern was reflected in his face. "Something's wrong," he said.

CHAPTER TWO

THE BOOK

Some people said he was the city's biggest sports bookie in more ways than one, because he handled the most betting action and also routinely tipped the scales at around 300 pounds. Bruce Weinstein was one of the busiest illegal sports bookies in Las Vegas, and he was also a formidable gambler, a high-roller who bet huge amounts of money on athletic events and played poker and other challenging games of chance and skill in casinos up and down the glittering entertainment corridor known all over the world as the Strip.

He was a big-time operator in his dual role as gambler and bookmaker, and he took his responsibilities to himself, his family, and his employees seriously. Bruce didn't mess around with drugs, and almost never drank anything alcoholic. A sip or two of wine during the holidays, or on some festive family occasion was all he would touch.

Gambling and running a sports book were Bruce's life, and he was good at them, because he'd grown up in the trade. His father, Fred White, had started the bookie business soon after the family moved to Los Angeles from their home in the tiny Catskill Mountain town of Liberty, New York, while Bruce was still a child. The Whites changed their names from Weinstein to match the name of an office-supply business they once owned before Fred realized that there was more money to be made in bookmaking. The bookie business was a profession Fred White had drifted into, and over time developed as a family operation.

By a curious twist of fate, one of the Los Angeles Police Department's leading experts on bookmaking was a native of the same little town in New York state where the Whites/ Weinsteins had once lived. John Paul Motto was a senior officer with the LAPD's Administrative Vice Division, which was responsible for overseeing the activities of eighteen divisional vice units operating throughout the city. It was Motto's job, and that of his colleagues with the AVD, to keep tabs on bookmakers and especially to keep a sharp eye out for any efforts by the Mafia or other elements of organized crime to muscle in on local gambling, prostitution, or pornography operations. Those are the criminal activities that most often provide the foot in the door for the Mob when it is attempting to move into new territory.

When Motto first began picking up information about Fred White, the former Liberty resident was still running a legitimate business that the officer later described to a Clark County, Nevada, grand jury during testimony in Las Vegas as being "sort of like . . . telemarketing . . . here he would start at 6 in the morning, and they were calling back east."

White's legitimate business calls usually kept him busy from about 6 a.m. to 2:30 p.m., Pacific Mountain Time, which was 9 a.m. to 5:30 p.m. on the East Coast. That meant White had all those telephones and long-distance lines unneeded for telemarketing and free from 2:30 in the afternoon, so, according to the senior vice cop, he put them to use in the bookmaking business.

Fred ran the operation and brought his sons, Bruce and Steven Weinstein, in with him, then gradually turned the business over to the boys, Motto said. It was always the LAPD's theory, the vice cop added, that Fred White was the money behind the operation, Bruce was the hands-on operator, and Steve stayed in the background handling payments and collections.

The New York state town of Liberty is isolated and small, about 4,500 year-round residents. So it isn't surprising that, on the rare occasions when former residents run into each other after moving away and following careers in larger metropolitan centers, a certain feeling of kinship often develops. That's the way it was when Bruce and Motto crossed professional paths in Los Angeles, even though it may seem that their jobs and careers would have made them natural enemies. They enjoyed sharing mutual experiences about their childhoods in the quiet little mountain settlement that was so different from the organized madness of the sprawling City of Angels.

Motto's specialty was bookies, and after working early in his career with divisional vice squads, where he learned how to develop informants and gather information, he attended courses on gambling at the FBI Academy in Quantico, Virginia, and taught his own course in bookmaking. He was well-trained, motivated, and street-smart.

The detective began receiving tips about Bruce from informants and vice squad cops in the districts in 1980, and passed on information to his superiors in weekly reports about the portly bookie's activities. Initially, Bruce wasn't doing enough business to justify the amount of preparation necessary to set up a bust by the AVD. It was up to detectives with the divisional vice squads to handle investigations involving small-timers like Bruce.

It was 1984 before Motto decided that Bruce was writing enough business to justify the personal attention of investigators with the Administrative Vice Division. He prepared a search warrant, and arrested Bruce for bookmaking. Through the 1980s and early 1990s, Motto or other vice squad cops in Los Angeles also arrested most of the members of Bruce's immediate family, including his parents, Fred and Sylvia White, his brother, Steven Marc Weinstein, and a sister, Robin Loehr.

Motto never personally worked up a case against Bruce again, although other vice squad officers in Los Angeles raided his bookie operations and arrested him several times. Bookmaking is classified as a felony under the California Criminal Code, but the courts tend to treat it as a misdemeanor and, unless there are extenuating circumstances, punishment is usually restricted to fines, probation, or very short prison terms. The arrests of members of the family bookmaking operation never led to jail time, but they were a nuisance and an expensive proposition.

The Weinstein/White business was conducted like most other illegal sports books. It was set up with from six to eight people, who worked in a house, garage, apartment, or office spaces that were big enough to accommodate a string of telephone lines.

Bruce was a natural-born bookie, who quickly became the brains of the operation. It was his responsibility to set the lines, by determining the point spreads for each game. In layman's terms, it was up to him to figure out how many runs or points a particular team was favored to win or lose by. The odds, or payoff rates, were based on the spread. It worked the same way in handicapping horse-racing; past records, track conditions, and other elements likely to affect the outcome were studied in order to set the odds.

During Bruce's later years operating the sports book in Los Angeles and eventually in Las Vegas, the betting office was also staffed with a manager-linesmaker, three or four clerks, and two or three additional employees. The clerks took the bets, which were phoned in from all over the country on prepaid 800-lines. Another employee took care of the board, keeping the various lines or point spreads up-to-date with information passed on to him or her from the linesmaker.

Experienced operators of sports books usually work from two locations: the main office where bets are accepted and recorded by people known as "front clerks," and the second location staffed by a "back clerk." The back clerk telephones the front office periodically through the day and makes a second record of the bets. When the information is relayed to the back office, the people in the front office destroy their records so that if there is a raid, the information can't be seized by the police.

When Motto led his lightning raid on the White/Weinstein bookmaking operation, the young bookie didn't have a back clerk, and admitted he was the boss. The police arrested everybody in the office, including Bruce and other members of his family, and seized all the records. The bookmaker had to spend a huge amount of money in a hurry so that he and his employees could get out of the courtroom and back into the betting office. Bail in raids on bookmakers was usually established at about $2,500 for each person arrested, and attorney fees and fines were piled on top. Finally, the location of the betting office had to be immediately changed after raids, adding to the expense. Moving the betting office around was necessary every few months or so anyway, to avoid attracting too much attention from neighbors and ultimately from the vice squad. A bust inevitably meant an early move, and a shakeup of the normal timetable.

It was all part of the business, and there were no hard feelings. It was the job of the White/Weinsteins to run a sports book. It was the job of Motto and other vice division detectives to see to it that things didn't get out of hand—things like the Mob moving in on the operation. The bookie and the vice officer quickly became friends of a sort, and developed a symbiotic relationship, similar to that of many professional criminals and cops. Bruce provided Motto with information.

"Bruce and I hit it off right away because he is from the same home town in upstate New York that I'm from," the chief of the LAPD's bookmaking operation later told the grand jury. The seasoned vice squad officer explained that he and his colleagues are more interested in milking bookies for information after arrests than in sending them to prison. "Our whole purpose is to sit the individual down and talk to them [sic] to try to find out what else is going on in town."

Motto and his partner sometimes stopped at Bruce's house for coffee and conversation on their way to work. They knew that he always got up early to set the lines, and they knew they could depend on the industrious bookie to give honest and complete answers when they asked questions.

If Motto asked, "Who are you playing with, Bruce? Anybody new in town?" he knew the bookie would bring him up-to-date with the latest information. With Bruce, Motto didn't need to prod, just ask.

Sometimes the cops and the bookie got together for an early dinner. The biggest problem Motto and his partner had with Bruce was keeping him from picking up the check. Motto and his pal repeatedly explained to him that, because they were cops and he was a bookie, they couldn't allow him to pay. But he kept trying, sometimes excusing himself to go to the men's room, then collaring the waiter and paying the bill ahead of time. The cops didn't let him get away with it.

Bruce was a sociable character, who was expansive and naturally friendly. If they were in a cocktail lounge where music was playing, he thought nothing of strolling over to a table occupied by two or three women, asking if he could buy a round of drinks, then inviting one of them to dance. A few minutes later the hefty gambler and the woman would be gliding around the dance floor. By the time shadows began to creep over the tops of the buildings outside, however, Bruce would be ready to head for home. He insisted on getting to bed early, because he had to be sharp for his work in the morning.

Despite the cozy relationship the rotund bookmaker developed with the LAPD bookmaking specialist, Bruce learned his lesson after the disastrous bust on his betting office, according to Motto. Bruce's sister Robin was assigned to the job of back clerk, so she could keep the records in a separate office. After a while Bruce also appointed an office manager and began using the telephone more often to keep in touch with his crew. For a few months he continued to come into the office for a couple of hours to set the lines and organize the day's work, but eventually handled virtually all of his business with employees by telephone.

In 1988, Bruce met a good-looking young woman named Elizabeth, and they were married about a year later in April 1989. She got pregnant on their honeymoon, and their daughter, Jaclyn, was born on January 24, 1990. Bruce was crazy about his little girl, but the domestic situation in the Weinstein household wasn't exactly peaches and cream.

One time when his wife was still pregnant, he lost his temper and hit her. She threatened to leave if he ever struck her again, and the physical abuse was never repeated.

There was no denying that the new husband earned an exceptionally good living. Elizabeth recalled years later that at one point during the marriage, Bruce's book was writing more than $1 million in business on weekends. The couple normally spent between $10,000 and $13,000 per month to maintain the household. Bruce drove a Mercedes convertible, and bought diamond jewelry, a new car, and other expensive gifts for his wife.

But Elizabeth wasn't satisfied. She later complained that he wasn't gracious about his gift-giving, and claimed it was always a struggle to get him to buy her anything. He was moody, took lithium, and for a time during their marriage was on Prozac. Although they had a joint bank account, he was always careful to deposit barely enough to pay the bills. If she wanted extra money, she had to work hard for it, especially if he was in a peevish mood.

It wasn't that he didn't have plenty of money lying around. Bruce routinely stashed thousands of dollars under the carpeting in their home, where it would be readily available when he needed money in a hurry. It was a good hiding place. He simply lifted up a corner of the carpet, cut out the matting so the bills would lie flat, then dropped the material back in place. At one time he had about $100,000 hidden there. Bookies justifiably worry about scrutiny of their finances by the Internal Revenue Service and other government or police agencies. So they tend to keep large amounts of cash on hand, and to put major purchases in the names of wives or other close relatives.

Bruce once explained to his wife that cash was a bookie's inventory, like clothes would be to the operators of boutiques or retail clothing stores. The couple lived very well, but he was careful about his inventory.

By 1991, however, after about two years of marriage, his wife decided that she was tired of living with Bruce Weinstein. She drove to the bank, cleaned the cash out of their safety deposit box, and left home with their daughter. There was considerable cash: $200,000 in $100 bills, all neatly wrapped in $10,000 stacks. The couple eventually agreed, without resorting to any court action, to divvy up the $200,000 by splitting it down the middle.

Bruce had good reasons for keeping large amounts of cash within easy reach, and they were more closely linked to his occupation as a gambler than as a bookie. Most successful bookies realize that the best way to get rich in the gaming business is by handling other people's bets, and avoid gambling with their own money. Bruce was an exception—he earned big money running the family book, and big money as a high-stakes gambler.

Like most gamblers, he had a system; but unlike most of the others', his system worked. When Bruce was placing money on a football, baseball, or basketball game, he bet the middle. Betting the middle wasn't unique, but he was more successful at it than most of his fellow gamblers. He kept a full-time employee busy calling other books around the country and offshore to the Dominican Republic and other Caribbean nations, checking the line or the point spread on games.

Sometimes, of course, the system didn't work and, like any bad-luck gambler, Bruce would be hung out to dry. On one exceptionally unlucky day, he reportedly dropped $100,000. Considering the emotional toll of a day like that, it's conceivable that some of the mood swings and peevishness that his ex-wife complained about were linked to the ups-and-downs of his gambling fortunes.

But Bruce knew his business, rigorously studied the

teams and the athletes, and had many more good days than bad. That was also true when he gambled in casinos. He loved the whole atmosphere of casino gambling: the muted rustle of cards being shuffled and dealt, the comforting click of dice tumbling over green felt-covered tables, and the tuxedoed male and female croupiers and dealers that were such vital elements of the beguiling Peter Pan promise of gold dust in the air.

After setting the lines, Bruce sometimes flew to Lake Tahoe to spend a few hours trying his luck at the tables and in the sports books. The popular resort on the huge lake that straddles the Nevada–California state line was one of his favorite places and he and a close friend took boating trips there whenever the time and opportunity were right. Bruce was a born chance-taker, with a bit of the daredevil in him, and as soon as the two men climbed into the boat he would steer into the choppiest water in the middle of the lake, even though the owners cautioned the landlubbers to stay close to shore.

Day trips to the glittering gambling spas weren't sufficiently satisfactory, however, and Bruce wanted to be closer to the action. An opportunity soon presented itself. Stories were making the rounds in official and unofficial circles that he was linked to a big-time California bookmaker who reputedly headed a multi-million-dollar operation with connections to a Caribbean betting syndicate. Bruce didn't appreciate that kind of attention, and he was anxious about the increasing scrutiny of Los Angeles cops. The City of Angels was becoming too crowded with bookies, anyway. Just before the beginning of the 1995 college and professional football season, he moved his sports book to Las Vegas.

Bruce's younger brother, Steve, stayed behind with his family in nearby Simi Valley, and their sister, Robin, also remained at her home in Moorpark. Steve continued to handle most of the payoff and collections—in bookmaking terms, the P and C side of the business.

Las Vegas was teeming with gamblers, so there was no problem staffing the new betting office. Bruce quickly settled on Brian Todd Foster as his office manager, and set up a betting operation in second-floor spaces over a window-screen store. Local vice squad officers quickly let him know that they were aware he was in town, and raided the office. Bruce reacted the way all professional books do: He paid his lawyers, paid his fines, and moved to a new location, this time to a little house on the 7400 block of Winterpine Avenue.

The house was in a residential area and looked like most of the other nearby homes, except for the half-dozen or so people who daily—weekdays and weekends—trooped inside between 7 and 8 a.m., and left almost exactly on the dot at 5 p.m. No one else ever entered the house. The sports book was a business whose customers never showed up at the office. Most of the clients were too far away for that, often hundreds or thousands of miles, and they called in their bets by telephone. Bettors didn't even know what city, state or country the book operated from.

The police raid didn't dampen the portly bookie's enthusiasm for Las Vegas in the slightest. Bruce loved living in the desert oasis and world gambling mecca, where the cards were dealt twenty-four hours a day every day, and the lights of the neon wilderness never dimmed. He was a jovial, free-spirited Falstaff, with a hearty sense of humor and a robust lust for life, who loved the excitement and the heady air of easy, seductive decadence that hung over the casinos of the city. Las Vegas was Bruce Weinstein's kind of town.

His parents had already lived in Las Vegas for more than

fifteen years, and he visited often, chatting about his daughter, Jaclyn, or about upcoming games and his luck with the horses, while playing with the Whites' three frisky white poodles in their comfortable Summerlin-area home. As always, he talked with his mother and father by phone at least twice a day.

When Bruce wasn't busy running his sports book, he was frequently at the dice or blackjack tables, or betting on the horses in one of the casinos on the Strip. Most often he was at the Stardust, Caesar's Palace, or the Mirage. Poker was one of his favorite games, and he especially liked playing in the poker room of the Mirage on Las Vegas boulevard, an institution among Las Vegas gamblers. When the casino opened in 1989, legendary poker player W. W. Boyd was dealt the ceremonial first hand. The longtime poker room manager at the Golden Nugget, Boyd initiated the practice of using house dealers to cut down on cheating, and won the five-card stud world series of poker five years in a row.

The Mirage poker room attracted high-rollers and low-limit players. Decorated with a Polynesian theme, the hotel and casino was internationally known for the thrilling performances of Siegfried and Roy, the magicians and animal trainers whose popular act features white tigers. But Bruce wasn't a tourist, he was a gambler, and he didn't go there for the shows.

Although his eyes were giving him trouble and it was becoming difficult for him to see the spots on the cards, he knew, as every good poker player does, that, although you have to play the hand you're dealt, the people who consistently win are those who know how to play the other players. When his opponents looked at their cards, Bruce watched for changes in their facial expressions, checked out body language, and listened for sudden sighs or other behavior likely to betray emotions.

Sometime in October 1995, the big man with the glasses, pencil mustache, and long white ponytail was playing $20 to $40 Texas Hold 'em at the Mirage when a friend introduced him to another player whose demeanor told him more than just what kind of cards she might be holding.

The poker player was a diminutive forty-seven-year-old woman with soft brown hair and come-hither blue eyes that seemed to be looking into his as often as they glanced at the cards in her hand. Everything about her body language and the easy, casual conversation they struck up while they sat side-by-side over the green felt of the poker table seemed to indicate that she was as interested in him as he was in her.

The woman's name was Amy DeChant, and the cards she would ultimately deal to Bruce Weinstein were aces and eights: the dead-man's hand.

CHAPTER THREE

THE GOLD DIGGER

"He never wanted anyone to bet what he couldn't
afford, and Bruce never harmed anyone."
—SYLVIA WHITE
COLUMN BY BOB SHEMELIGIAN
LAS VEGAS SUN

Amy Rica DeChant was petite, but she was a grown-up
woman of the world, who had bounced around the country
living here and there with this man and that before landing
in Las Vegas in 1992.

Her love life was about as unstable as one of the dried-
up tumbleweeds that twist and skid across the sand and
gravel of the desert on the outskirts of the city, hesitating
for a while in one location before suddenly catching a
breeze or a sudden gust of wind and once more moving on.

It seemed that she simply wasn't capable of keeping a
serious love affair going for very long, although she had a
remarkable ability to maintain close friendships with old
sweethearts long after the fire of their romance had dwin-
dled and died. Amy's romances didn't sour because of any
lack of ability to charm a man and make him fall in love,
or remain in love, with her. She had that skill in abundance.
The problem was tied to something else that lurked deep
inside of her own psyche.

It may be that Amy's butterfly affairs can be traced to her childhood and young adult years, which are still hazy and perplexing to police and other investigators who have peered into her life and examined the complex personality quirks and failings that created the dangerously devious woman she became. Despite all they learned, and everything that was eventually developed and exposed in the courtroom, she is still very much of a mystery woman.

She had used different names, and exhibited a confounding tangle of personalities during her checkered career as a businesswoman and alluring *femme fatale*. Some of the people who should be the best informed about her can't even agree about her height or how much she weighs. She has been described in a courtroom as a diminutive five-oot, one-inch tall, 110-pound woman, but some police reports indicate she is five-foot, three and place her weight at 120. That's the way it is with Amy DeChant: nothing can be taken for granted, not even the most routine factor or event.

Amy was born in a Newark, New Jersey, hospital, on March 19, 1948. Her first name is of Latin and French origin, and means "beloved" or "loved," which in view of later events appears to have been ironically prescient. In astrological terms, she was born under the sign of Pisces, the fish; her element is water and her planet is Neptune. Bruce Weinstein shared the same signs, although he was born almost two full years after Amy, on March 1, 1950.

As a baby, Amy lived with her family in Fords, New Jersey, between Perth Amboy and New Brunswick. She told Sylvia White and other members of Bruce's family that she was a child when her mother was placed in a mental hospital. By the time she was sixteen, after the death of her father, she was on her own. Other tales have circulated that she was adopted by a couple who were settled on Florida's southeast coast. By the time Amy began frequenting Las

Vegas's Strip casinos, she was a woman whose past was already shrouded in mystery.

Based on Amy's track record and spotty romantic history, by the time she became a young adult, she knew exactly what she wanted out of life, and she also seems to have figured out how to get it: through hard work—and if that didn't do the job, by taking advantage of the weaknesses and gullibility of vulnerable men.

Amy was good with men. She was a seductive Lorelei, an irrepressible temptress who seemed instinctively to know how to manipulate and control males. She wasn't knockout beautiful, but she was nice-looking and knew how to put to best use every single feminine wile in her personal arsenal to attract and hold them. And although she traveled through parts of the Midwest and along the Atlantic Coast all the way to south Florida, the pull of her New Jersey roots repeatedly drew her back to the Garden State.

She was in New Jersey in 1985 when she strolled into the office of John Gerard, the property manager at the Regency Manor Apartments in New Brunswick, and introduced herself as a general contractor looking for work. She said she wanted to repair the roofs and take care of some of the other maintenance jobs at the complex. Gerard needed help and her prices were reasonable, so he agreed. She had her own foreman and crew, and they worked on four or five buildings, repairing or replacing roofs, installing windows, and taking on various other jobs. Amy handled all the paperwork, scouted out jobs for the fledgling business, and provided the overall supervision.

The property manager soon learned that his new contractor was living in the apartments with one of the older residents, George Sackel. Amy's boyfriend was about twenty-five years older than she was and owned Aaction Sackel Moving and Storage in nearby Perth Amboy, a company he had started and built up over the years. Sackel was financially comfortable and his relationship with the younger woman seemed to be solid and warm.

Sackel didn't know that his live-in girlfriend had begun slipping out on dates with the property manager. The affair between Gerard and Amy didn't last long, but she soon had another secret lover with whom she was cheating on her older boyfriend. By 1987 Sackel learned that Amy was carrying on an affair with her foreman, and the May–December romance finally went down the tubes. The couple quarreled, but eventually agreed to a reasonably amicable settlement, and parted on a friendly basis. Gerard heard that Amy and Sackel had sold a house and divided things up between them. During the long-term relationship Amy had seen to it that her sweetheart put much of the property in her name, and she was left very well off.

Sackel was heart-broken after Amy ran off to Detroit with her foreman, and she was so concerned about his welfare that she asked Gerard to keep an eye on the older man. Gerard had already met Sackel a few times while Amy was contracting maintenance work at the apartments and liked him. The two men quickly became close friends.

Even though they had broken off their brief fling long ago, Gerard and Amy also continued to maintain their friendship. Amy was a fascinating companion, who could rapidly metamorphose from a deliciously tempting sex-pot, to an irrepressible madcap, or to a no-nonsense, hard-nosed businesswoman. She danced through as many business projects as she did boyfriends, and at times juggled multiple ventures on both fronts.

While she was still living in New Jersey and seeing a lot of Gerard, she combined business and romance for a while. She set up a professional escort service, and gave her friend a handful of cards to pass out to any of his pals or contacts who might be looking for a charming female companion for an hour or so. She didn't say if the services involved sharing more than an innocent dinner, a theater date, or a social gathering with the client's business associates, but Gerard figured that if the customer wanted something more intimate Amy would see to it that it was available.

While they were hanging around together, Gerard also met her brother, Michael A. "Mickey" Gerber, who lived in the New Brunswick area. In addition to his work at the apartment complex, Gerard operated a cabinet business, and Gerber helped him make important business contacts at the giant Johnson & Johnson Company. Gerber was a longtime employee there.

After Amy's breakup with Sackel, she stayed in touch with Gerard, telephoning from Detroit or other cities, and stopped by to see him or called and chatted for a few minutes during frequent visits with her brother in New Jersey. Sometimes she stopped by the Regency Manor or met Gerard at a restaurant to have dinner with him. She always asked how George was doing.

Amy had mentioned that she had another brother somewhere in New England, but Mickey was clearly her favorite. Their close relationship apparently had a lot to do with her habit of shuttling back and forth between New Jersey and wherever else her wanderings led her.

Her romance with the foreman dissolved soon after they moved to Michigan, and for a while she resettled in Ohio. But by 1992, she had discovered Las Vegas and moved there to continue following the twin obsessions of her life: money and men. She soon developed a love for gambling, although she was never a high-roller. Amy worked too hard for her money for that, and when she ventured into the casinos as a player it was generally to try her luck at low-limit poker tables.

Like many people who move to Las Vegas from out-of-state looking for opportunities, Amy found work in the casinos. She started as a croupier and card dealer, steadily expanding her knowledge of the gaming business, while continuing to attract and charm a succession of men. While she was working as an extra poker dealer at the old Vegas World, she struck up a close friendship with the poker room supervisor, Roy Seider. Seider was a fifty-year-old native of New Jersey and they took an immediate liking to each other, frequently reminiscing about their home state. They provided moral support for each other during lean times, and on some occasions when Seider was short of cash she paid for dinner or loaned him a few dollars to tide him over until payday. Seider liked her. She was hard-working and, from what he had seen of her, a good-hearted, loyal friend.

Men usually took to Amy. She knew how to make them feel good about themselves. She liked the things they liked, and talked their talk. Although Amy also had women friends, many of her female colleagues in the casinos were less entranced than their male counterparts were ·with her vivacious, bubbly personality. One woman who had worked with her in a casino told the *Las Vegas SUN* years later, "She's too sweet—the type that's always smiling." She was too constantly sunny for their liking, and they thought she was a phony who was playing a role.

But Amy's smiles and spritely personality worked like a charm with most men, and she expertly glided through a steady procession of boyfriends while continuing to dabble in a variety of small business ventures. The pixie-faced vixen with the shoulder-length rusty hair was working as a poker dealer at the Primadonna Resorts in nearby Stateline when she started dating Keith Leroy Bower, the newly divorced shift supervisor in the poker room.

They never moved in together and the romance quickly fizzled out. Amy told Bower that he didn't have enough money to keep her, but, as she did with so many of her ex-sweethearts, she replaced romance with friendship. It wasn't easy for a man to get Amy out of his system, and she and Bower continued to chat occasionally even after she'd moved on to other boyfriends and other jobs.

It was more difficult for her to stay in close touch with another former boyfriend after they parted company, because he was locked up in a California prison serving a lengthy sentence for drug trafficking. He had a private pilot's license and stories were circulating around Las Vegas that he was involved in shady dealings before he ran afoul of the law in California for flying cocaine into the country. The pilot had had a nice home on a golf course in Las Vegas before he met Amy, and gave her power of attorney so she could help him with appeals and other post conviction affairs. Then Amy, who wasn't personally linked to any drug-dealing or drug-using, got into trouble herself.

Amy had started her own business, DeChant & Company Carpet Cleaning, when she met Michael Anthony Lucarelli in the early fall of 1994. The handsome, forty-two-year-old man was the general manager of the sales force at Carriage Car auto sales when she walked into his Fremont street office with a business proposition. She wanted to work out a deal to clean car seats for Carriage.

Lucarelli wasn't interested, but she showed up a week later with the same proposal. He still wasn't willing to reconsider the earlier decision, so she waited another week and approached him again. The manager was sitting at his desk when she walked up behind him and started rubbing his back. The impromptu massage was soothing, and when she added that she would like to go out with him sometime, Lucarelli relented. The company actually did have some cars with upholstery that could use a good cleaning, so he agreed to give her a chance to show what she could do.

Having DeChant and Company clean dirty upholstery, rather than ripping it out and replacing it, made good economic sense. Amy did much of the cleaning herself, with help from a single male employee.

But demand for her services was spotty. A few weeks after she talked the sales manager into the service agreement, Amy telephoned and invited him over to her home in an apartment complex off Lake Mead Drive. Soon after the first visit, he moved into her condominium with her.

The romance lasted longer than DeChant & Company's stint at Carriage. Lucarelli's boss didn't like the quality of the work she was doing and cancelled the handshake agreement she had with the sales manager. A few weeks later, Lucarelli also left Carriage and went to work for his girlfriend.

DeChant & Company had some new contracts: sprucing up the upholstery on some of the aircraft flying into McCarran International Airport on Wayne Newton Boulevard, and cleaning the green felt surfaces of blackjack, poker and dice tables in some Strip casinos. Amy kept busy with management and sales, and Lucarelli worked as her full-time employee, operating the cleaning machines. A woman also worked part-time cleaning the interiors of some of the airplanes for Scenic and for Eagle Airlines during busy periods.

Lucarelli quickly mastered the techniques for using the tools of the trade, including knowledge of the various chemicals necessary for different cleaning jobs. Amy explained how to use degreasers, acetone, and various other compounds and liquids. Some of the solutions, especially acetone, were caustic, and Lucarelli wore a mask and gloves when he used them to do a job.

Amy didn't talk much about her finances, but she was making a good living. In his testimony to the grand jury, Lucarelli later described her as "a hustler. She was excellent sales, excellent. She would latch onto an account and just pursue it and pursue it. A lot of tenacity . . . She never took 'no' for an answer." She was also a woman who was convinced that she knew everything and had all the answers, he said.

Amy was on a roll, and life was good. She drove an old Cadillac, had collected some valuable jewelry, owned a rental house and a condominium in another part of the city, houses or condominium apartments in Michigan and Florida, and her business was flourishing.

But she didn't have long discussions with her boyfriend about her financial affairs. Lucarelli's financial achievements were more modest. After taxes and other expenses, he cleared about $400 to $500 per week, depending on the amount of work that was available. The couple had been living and working together about eighteen months when Amy began to put new strains on the business and the relationship. They lost the job cleaning gaming tables at the MGM Grand Hotel Casino on South Las Vegas Boulevard, which was their biggest account. New men were appearing in her life and she was cutting back on her sales promotion activities. There were other ways to acquire wealth, and Amy concluded that her live-in boyfriend would never be able to provide her with the kind of lifestyle she desired. She couldn't see any future together, she told him. Money, or more precisely, Lucarelli's lack of money, was an important factor in their relationship.

His romance with Amy burned itself out after only eight or nine months. By mutual agreement, Lucarelli moved out during the late summer of 1995, but continued to work for his former girlfriend even after he met and married another woman.

Amy was too busy pursuing her new interests and wasn't lining up enough work to keep Lucarelli busy, or his earnings at their previous levels. His paychecks soon took a nosedive. The drop in income was especially badly timed for a newly married man, and he had other troubles as well. His new wife, Katie, didn't like the idea of the close business relationship he still had with his former girlfriend. Lucarelli finally decided that the strain on his income and his marriage was simply too much to put up with, and found another job.

Amy had managed to hold onto a contract to clean restaurant chairs at the MGM, and Lucarelli trained his replacement—a poker-playing grandfather named Bobby Wayne Jones—there. Then he turned over the cleaning machines, the chemicals, and the worn, two-tone light brown company van to Jones and stepped out of the picture.

Even while Amy was living with Lucarelli, she had continued to carry on flirtations and hit-and-run romances with various men she met through her business and her activities around the gaming tables. She was constantly on the prowl. For a while, one of her conquests was Robert Moon, a bartender working the swing shift in the Hacienda bar at the Las Vegas Hilton Hotel and Casino while she cleaned dice and blackjack tables there. As with so many of her love affairs, the romance didn't last long, but they remained friends.

Late in 1995 Amy stopped at the Hacienda and boasted to Moon that she had a new boyfriend, a big-shot bookie with the kind of money necessary to take care of a woman like her. The bartender asked what she was doing with her condominium on the west side of town. She said she'd sold it when she moved in with her new beau.

Amy showed off a snazzy turquoise Z-28 Chevy Camaro convertible with a black top to another old flame, Keith Bower, when she dropped in to see him at the poker room in the Primadonna. She told the poker room shift supervisor that it had been given to her by her rich new boyfriend.

Amy also talked with Lucarelli and told him she had finally found the man of her dreams. He was a bookie, who was loaded with money. His name was Bruce Weinstein.

CHAPTER FOUR

THE DOMESTIC LIFE

Amy and Bruce had clicked almost immediately, from the moment their eyes first met across the poker table at the Mirage. That was shortly before Halloween. By Christmas, they were living together in his rented apartment.

Early in January 1996, Amy supervised a move into a luxurious new 4,280-square-foot custom-built home inside a gated community called the Castle Vista Estates on the southwest edge of the city. The two-story, Spanish-style stucco structure at 5452 Castle Vista Court had a living room, dining room, kitchen, one bedroom, a bathroom, and an office downstairs. Three more bedrooms, each with its own bath and balcony, a family room, and office were upstairs. The Las Vegas skyline could be viewed glittering in the distance from huge picture windows. The house had a fireplace, and the back yard was dominated by a spacious swimming pool. Bruce arranged to have the pool heated so Amy could swim year-round.

Bruce had one of the bays of the attached three-car garage modified and fixed up as a separate office with a computer and telephone lines. There was still plenty of room for his gleaming gold-colored Lincoln and for Amy's 1995 Camaro. Kenny Reisch, an employee who telephoned other bookies to check out the lines as part of Bruce's personal gambling operation, worked in the office. He also lived at the house and occupied the downstairs bedroom.

The handsome red-tile–roofed stucco was one of fourteen homes platted in the luxury complex, all but three eventually constructed by custom home–builder Yohan Lowie. Bruce's house was one of the first that Lowie sold. The exclusive gated community was shut off from the outside world by a solid block wall built all the way around the property.

Bruce was still living in California, but had already decided to move to Las Vegas when he first met Lowie. The home-builder owned some properties in the northwest area of town that Bruce checked out, but none of them were what he was looking for. After scouting out possible homes for ten months and still failing to find what he wanted, Bruce agreed to Lowie's offer to build a custom house for him. The husky gambler had his own conceptions about how it should be constructed, and shared his ideas about design and certain security features with the builder. Bruce's mother sat in on a couple of the talks about the construction plans, but for the most part Bruce called the shots. The builder and the buyer settled on the location, and Lowie went to work erecting Bruce's new home on an approximate half-acre plot.

Luxury and security were two features Bruce insisted on, and Lowie saw to it that his client, who was also becoming a close friend, got exactly what he wanted. Bruce didn't spare the expense. At his instruction, Lowie installed about $100,000 worth of marble, including a marble book bench, marble ceilings, and marble steam showers, with fixtures of stainless steel. None of the flooring was ceramic tile. According to Bruce's wishes, it was all marble and granite.

Bruce demanded an equally elaborate and expensive security system. Installing such a sophisticated system was a new experience for Lowie, and after investigating the problem, he called in one of the best professionals in the business to take care of the job.

Joseph Corbin owned the Central Alarm company, and had worked in sales and installation of security systems in Las Vegas for about fifteen years when he was contracted to protect Bruce's home. Corbin also put in the vacuum system inside the house, installing six outlets in different rooms or hallways. The home automation system was state-of-the-art, and turned Bruce's home into a "smart house." Bruce could call on a touch-tone telephone from anywhere in the world and flick the lights on or off, in the house or in the pool and spa, or activate or deactivate the alarm system. In addition to motion detectors and audible alarms, video cameras were linked to the system monitoring the front door and back exits, and he could watch the pictures they produced through any of the nine television sets in the house. The cameras could be operated to show views of the front and back yards, as well as a large area of the street in front of the house. If someone rang the doorbell, Bruce or Amy could check the visitor out on television before answering the door.

A less dramatic but more unusual feature of the house was a square hole that Bruce had asked Lowie to cut into the drywall inside the master bedroom closet. Crude and primitive compared to the technological wonders of the security system, the square was designed to function as Bruce's in-home safe to store cash or other valuables.

It wasn't a real safe, but it was ingenious and practical.

There was no locking mechanism or any metal parts that might be detectable by a burglar or some other thief carrying special metal-detecting equipment. The builder concealed the secret compartment under a heavy cabinet. Only Bruce and Lowie would know the cut-out safe was there.

Among other conventional fixtures, Lowie installed a special knob and screw on the cabinet, designed to be turned sideways in a certain manner to open the compartment. He also added a special touch of his own to protect the hiding place, by sticking a few fake electrical wires around the drywall cut-out. They weren't hooked up to anything electrical, but they were thick red, yellow, and black wires that looked like they carried high-voltage current, and were counted on to discourage snoopers.

Before emigrating to the United States almost ten years earlier, the custom home–builder had served in the Israeli Army where, among other skills, he developed expertise as a light armament specialist. Lowie was experienced with details involving security and concealment, and had previously constructed safe rooms, safe basements, and capsules in houses for other clients.

Bruce was romantically unencumbered when he first arranged with Lowie to build the house, and he settled into a rented apartment after moving to town. By the time the house was ready to be occupied, however, Amy had become his live-in girlfriend and they moved into the new home the same day that Lowie obtained the certificate of occupancy. The security system was already hooked up and working when they moved in. Amy was the only one who knew the code—Bruce didn't even know it—and she took care of switching the alarm on or off.

Amy was suddenly mistress of a brand-new home with a value estimated at around $675,000, including more than $343,000 paid to the builder and thousands of dollars in additional costs for security, marble and other special amenities. Bruce was seeing to it that she lived very well. It seemed she had at last found a man who could take care of her in the style she had always desired. Thanks to her rich boyfriend, Amy was driving a shiny late-model leased convertible, and she ordered a vanity license plate that read, "HI ON BRC." It was a nice touch that was typically Amy. She knew how to make a man feel special and good about himself.

Bruce also bought her an expensive diamond necklace, a printer for her business, and other gifts, and took her along on out-of-state holidays or long weekend trips. They vacationed in Florida, where Bruce's grandmother lived, went to California several times, and on one occasion spent a few days in Mesquite on the Nevada–Arizona border, a desert oasis of about one thousand residents that was developing into a resort. Amy'd wanted to spend some time at Players Island, a popular casino there.

Bruce's size wasn't a hindrance to their romance, although she wanted him to lose weight for his own good. Moon was a big man, and she had dated or lived with other boyfriends who were grossly overweight, so she knew what to do. She started working on Bruce to get him to melt off some of his excess pounds. It made sense because he was diabetic, which may have had something to do with his difficulty making out the spots on the cards when he played poker. Now that Amy had at last found a man who could afford to keep her in the style she felt she deserved, she didn't want to lose him to a diabetic stroke or a heart attack.

On the surface, it may have appeared that they were good for each other. Bruce's parents were pleased that his new girlfriend was getting him to take better care with his diet, and to exercise regularly. Thanks in part to Amy's prodding, he swam a lap or two every day in the sparkling water of the pool in back of the house. Within six or seven months of the time they began living together, Bruce had trimmed forty pounds off his five-foot, nine-inch frame and was down to about 260.

While Bruce was making time for exercise, Amy kept him happy with regular doses of lovemaking. They practiced bedroom acrobatics five or six times a day, according to one of the people who was eventually called on to track her activities. Amy knew how to keep a man happy. In addition to her enthusiastic lovemaking skills, she was a fine amateur masseuse and she moved her own professional massage table into the house. She gave Bruce regular massages and rubdowns to relax him and get him feeling better after an exhausting day on the telephones and in the casinos.

Their relationship wasn't all peaches and cream, however. Although Bruce bought her nice presents, he didn't give her money, and they didn't open any joint bank accounts. He also refused to invest in any businesses in her name, or to buy her property—but it wasn't because of a lack of effort on her part.

They had only been seeing each other a couple of months when Amy, Bruce, and his mother stopped in a bagel shop at the corner of Tropicana and Jones, near the Castle Vista Estates where the new home was still under construction. Bruce told his mother that a bar and gaming establishment just around the corner was for sale; it had video gambling machines in it, and he was thinking of buying it and putting it in Amy's name. Bruce didn't like putting things in his own name because of the particular businesses he was in. He had already put the house at 5452 Castle Vista Court in Robin's name, and even his credit card was registered to his brother Steven. As a known bookie with an arrest record, he couldn't obtain a business and gaming license, so Amy would have to be the owner of record. Mrs. White asked her son how he could think of doing that. "We don't even know this girl," she reminded him. Bruce didn't buy the bar.

Two or three months after moving into the new house, Amy talked to Bruce's mother about another business venture she was interested in. She wanted Bruce to put up $150,000 to buy a nursing or retirement home and put it in her name so federal tax authorities wouldn't be tipped off to his big expenditure. Mrs. White didn't like the idea. She explained to her son and his girlfriend that liability insurance for a business like that would be a backbreaking burden. Bruce didn't put up the money, and the venture was dropped.

So Amy came up with another proposal. Fred White was experiencing health problems and Bruce wanted to buy his parents a nearby custom house in the same tract as his, where it would be more convenient for him to watch over them. He had already begun negotiations to purchase the plot when the family got together at the Texas Steakhouse with the realtor to discuss the mortgage. They had barely begun to talk about the project when Amy turned to Mrs. White and said: "Would you ask Bruce if he would put half the house in my name?"

Mrs. White was shocked by the suggestion. "I can't ask him to put half of my house in your name," she replied. Bruce agreed with his mother. They figured the house should be in the name of the baby of the family, Robin, not Amy. Amy was furious, and stormed out of the restaurant.

Jaclyn visited regularly with her father and grandparents in Las Vegas, and her mother—whose new married name was Elizabeth Tuch—and Amy began sharing their mutual criticisms of Bruce when Mrs. Tuch telephoned to discuss the girl's care. They talked often during Jaclyn's visits because, as the woman of the house, Amy assumed primary responsibility for taking care of the spirited six-year-old and monitoring her bedtime and other activities.

Elizabeth later recalled a remark by Amy that in retrospect was exceedingly ominous. The two women were comparing Bruce's shortcomings as a husband or boyfriend, raking him over the coals because he slept naked, snored, was verbally abusive, and was a tightwad. When Amy complained that Bruce didn't give her any money, Elizabeth asked: "Then what are you doing with him? I hate to sound crass like that, but you know, what are you doing with him?"

Amy replied: "I have my own agenda."

Mrs. Tuch, who later recounted the conversation in testimony, said she was baffled by the cryptic remark. She couldn't understand why Amy was staying with Bruce if he was so abusive and stingy. "She wasn't married to him; she didn't have any children with him; there was no reason for her to stay," the woman said.

Amy also bitched about Bruce's stingy ways to Elizabeth's brother, Shawn Hallman. Hallman made frequent visits to Bruce's home and Amy felt comfortable enough with him to share confidences about her money troubles. One time as they were walking across the street to Lowie's home to pick up a nail to install a temperature gauge, she began complaining about how difficult it was to live with Bruce and to put up with his bad moods and tightfistedness. She griped about his refusal to buy the bar for her and said he never gave her any money. She conceded that he had offered to buy her clothes, but said she'd refused the offers.

Hallman thought the bitching sounded a lot like stories he had heard before from his sister. "If it's that bad, you should leave him," he suggested. "You know, otherwise, why would you stay with someone if you weren't getting along?" The young man later recalled that Amy replied by saying something about having an idea for working it out, although he couldn't remember the exact words.

Elizabeth Tuch and Shawn Hallman weren't the only people Amy complained to about Bruce's alleged stinginess. After moving in with the bookie, she continued to talk periodically with her former boyfriend Lucarelli, and griped that Bruce was so miserly, he not only wouldn't give her any money, but she had to pay her own bills. He took her to dinner and to shows, but there were no cash gifts, even though he gambled huge amounts of money. She also whined that he was verbally abusive to her. Lucarelli later recalled during grand jury testimony that Bruce's tight-fistedness "kind of pissed her off."

She told Lucarelli about trying to get Bruce to buy the bar and put it in her name because he had had troubles with the law that would make it impossible for him to get a gaming license. Early in 1996, when Lucarelli was working for a local auto dealer, Amy told him that Bruce was going to buy her a car, and she took a red Acura Integra out for a test drive. She brought the car back a couple of hours later and told him that Bruce couldn't fit inside and didn't like it, so the deal went down the drain. Lucarelli provided professional advice about negotiating with another car dealer after Amy told him that Bruce was thinking about buying or leasing a Lexus for her. She said she had definitely decided that that was the kind of car she wanted, but figured a Lexus would cost about $49,000 or $50,000, and the only way she could afford it was if Bruce paid for it. The deal for the Lexus also fell through.

At the beginning of July, Jaclyn was just settling in at the new house on Castle Vista Court to spend the entire month with her father and paternal grandparents. Bruce always tried to plan his schedule so he could spend as much time with her as possible, and had set up a fun trip to Lake Tahoe. They planned to leave on Sunday and spend three days at the exciting lakeside gambling resort. They had purchased their airplane tickets, and Amy was already packing.

CHAPTER FIVE

ACES AND EIGHTS

Everyone at the book on Winterpine was worried about Bruce.

Bruce's failure to call the office and set the lines Saturday morning, and Foster's inability to locate him was more than disturbing. The sense of dread that had been dogging Mrs. White turned to alarm.

If Bruce wasn't already dead, it appeared that he was badly hurt or in serious trouble, and being held by someone who was preventing him from getting in touch with his family and his employees.

Sylvia White had worried ever since her eldest son failed to telephone her at home earlier that morning, and her misgivings increased after he hadn't made his usual calls to his office manager.

The last time she'd spoken with him was Friday night. He always telephoned at least once for a quick chat before going to bed, and Friday he'd called twice. He'd gone to the Friday night races earlier in the evening and wanted to say goodnight to his daughter Jaclyn.

Another granddaughter was visiting from California, and Sylvia had invited the girls to stay overnight, because she didn't want to burden Amy with the care of two children while Bruce was out. Mrs. White had taken the girls to Pistol Pete's for rides and pizza, so when Bruce telephoned the first time at about 8:30 p.m., his daughter wasn't there. Fred White answered the phone, and the father and son chatted for a few minutes about the races and other matters before Bruce hung up.

When Mrs. White returned home a short time later with the girls, she telephoned her son, then put his daughter on the line so Bruce could say goodnight to her. He didn't say anything during the conversations with his parents or with his daughter about going out again Friday evening.

Shaken, the silver-haired grandmother telephoned Reisch and asked if Bruce's Lincoln was parked in the garage. He confirmed that it was, but couldn't tell her anything about Bruce that he hadn't already told Foster. So Sylvia hung up and immediately dialed the house again on another line. Amy answered, and Mrs. White asked to speak with her son. Amy said that he'd left the house at about 11 o'clock Friday night and hadn't returned.

Mrs. White then asked, "If Bruce isn't home, is his car home?" Amy said it was. The worried mother already knew something was dreadfully out of kilter, and the information about Bruce's Lincoln deepened her sense of dread. Bruce wouldn't go anyplace without his car.

She was so upset, she telephoned Steven in Simi Valley, and told him what was going on. "There's something wrong," she said. "I don't know what's wrong, but there's something wrong." Bruce's sudden vanishing sounded as ominous to Steven as it did to his mother, and he told her he would catch the first available flight to Las Vegas.

Later Saturday afternoon Mrs. White and her husband

drove to the Castle Vista Estates to try and sort out some of the answers to the mystery that had so suddenly intruded upon their lives. The Whites had their own key and let themselves inside before slipping off their shoes and leaving them in the marble entryway. Bruce's sandals were nearby. Mrs. White called out to Amy, and she answered back, saying that she was upstairs.

The Whites began walking upstairs and were near the landing when Sylvia stepped on wet carpeting. Peering down toward her stockinged feet, she saw brownish stains around the wet spot. Stooping down, she brushed at the spot with a finger, then lifted it to her nose. It smelled like vinegar—like someone had been cleaning.

Amy was in the master bedroom, and when Mrs. White walked in and asked what she was doing, she replied that she had a pile of washing to do because of the Lake Tahoe trip scheduled for the next day.

The worried older woman didn't feel good about the way the bedroom looked. Amy was a good housekeeper who made up the bed every morning, and the quilts and pillows were tastefully coordinated with the window coverings. But the quilt and pillows were all stripped from the bed, and only a sheet covered the blue-and-white–patterned mattress. Mrs. White was even more disturbed when she noticed her son's cellular phone, sports pager, and American Express card lying in plain sight on the dresser. The Whites knew that the phone, the pager, and the credit card were essential to Bruce's work, and he always carried them with him when he went out. Bruce's diabetes medicine was his other essential, and Amy said he'd taken it with him.

She told the anxious parents that Bruce had left the house at 11 o'clock the previous evening and handed her the credit card, instructing her to go on to Lake Tahoe with

Jaclyn if he wasn't back in time to take the same flight. He'd promised to meet them there later. Fred White asked what his son was wearing when he left, and Amy said he was dressed in shorts and had sandals on his feet. The Whites knew that Bruce had only one pair of sandals, because his feet were so wide that it was difficult to find others that fit.

Steven arrived from California with his wife and son late that afternoon, and the family met at Bruce's house. It was a dismal gathering, and the Whites and Weinsteins feared the worst. There was no doubt in their minds that something terrible had happened to Bruce. Amy spent most of the time after Steven's arrival sitting outside in a chaise chair, while family members worried and tried to figure out what was going on. A few tears misted in her eyes and trickled down her cheeks.

Steven's wife, Jamie, at last said she was tired, and the family members decided to return to the White home. Amy was still outside, and Mrs. White asked if she would like to come with them instead of remaining in the big house by herself. The younger woman agreed, and stuffed some clothes into a small overnight bag, then filled a pillowcase with other items. She drove her own car. When she entered the Whites' house, she brought the overnight bag, but left the pillowcase and its mysterious contents outside in the Camaro.

Amy's behavior continued to be disturbingly out of keeping with the situation. Bruce's family members were heartsick, and their dread and discomfort hung like a shroud over the tastefully furnished home, that was filled with photographs of family weddings, children and grandchildren. No one knew what to do and no one wanted to go to bed. No one except Amy! She was clearly exhausted, and staggered off to bed only a few minutes after everyone arrived at the house.

The Whites talked things over with Steven and decided to file a missing persons report with the Las Vegas Metro Police Department. Amy didn't seem to be in any rush to report Bruce missing, so they had to take things in their own hands. They agreed to file the report on Sunday morning. At about 7:30 they decided to go out to dinner, woke Amy up, and invited her to go along. They told her about the decision to report Bruce as a missing person, and she said she wanted to go to the police station with them.

Amy immediately went to bed again after they returned to the house following dinner, and other family members eventually followed suit. Almost everyone had trouble sleeping, and they tossed and turned or lay there with their eyes open, repeatedly reviewing the events of the day and running various scenarios through their minds. Mrs. White didn't sleep at all, and she was out of bed by 6 a.m. All the adults were up by 7 a.m., including Amy, who surprised everyone by announcing that she had to leave for a while.

Steven reminded her that he wanted to file the missing persons report as soon as possible. Amy indicated that she understood and promised to meet him at 9 a.m. at Bruce's house. Steven and his mother were at the house at 9 o'clock, but Amy wasn't there, and she didn't telephone. At 9:30, Steven left to go to the police station by himself and file the report. Sylvia stayed behind to wait for Amy, who showed up about a half-hour later toting a couple of small grocery bags. She explained to Bruce's mother that she'd had to pick up groceries, because there was hardly any food in the house due to the earlier plans to leave for Lake Tahoe that day.

Amy left to meet Steven at a nearby police substation, but it was closed on Sundays, so she drove to the main offices downtown. Steven had finally walked into the police station shortly before 11 a.m., to talk with a police officer about the missing gambler. Amy showed up while he was there, and was listed on the official report with him as filing the missing persons complaint. Concise and to the point, the initial report read:

Missing person/possible homicide.
Subject: Division reporting, ISD, date and time oc-curred 7–05–96 23:30.
Location of occurance[sic]. 5452 Castle Vista Court, 89118.
Victim: Weinstein, Bruce Charles.
LVMPD ID #: 618389. WMA.
DOB: 03–01–50.
5'9", 260, white/haz.
LSW [last seen wearing]: Navy slacks and sandals.
5452 Castle Vista Court, Las Vegas. Self-employed professional gambler.

Larry Hanna, a sergeant with almost twenty years' ex-perience with the Metro police department, including three years as a detective with the Missing Persons Division, was assigned to the case. In a later typewritten report detailing action taken on the case Hanna wrote that, although the family viewed the bookie's disappearance as suspicious, "the information produced did not lend itself to any indi-cation of suspicious circumstances nor foul play." The in-vestigator said that he suggested the family contact credit-card companies doing business with Bruce to watch for any current transactions, and review his telephone bills for out-of-state contacts.

Hanna also noted that the family suspected Amy had something to do with Bruce's disappearance, and they explained that "he could be very abrasive and may have upset her to the point she may have shot him and gained assistance in removing and concealing the body." Hanna wrote that the report was filed by Bruce's brother, Steven Weinstein, and by Amy, the missing man's "significant other."

Despite his observation about the lack of evidence of foul play, Hanna began the routine, turning over rocks and peering into dark corners, looking for clues to the missing man's whereabouts. One of the first things he did was contact the Metro police department's pawn detail, and quickly confirmed that neither Bruce nor Amy had any firearms registered to them.

Even though Missing Persons was on the case, it was obvious that the entire police department wasn't going to drop everything else and turn all their attention to looking for a vanished bookie who was a grown man. That may have seemed to be especially true because of his profession, which presumably would bring him into occasional contact with shady characters who weren't known for advertising their activities.

The Whites and Steven Weinstein decided to hire a private detective to find Bruce. Bruce's manager, Brian Foster, told the Whites that he had a friend at the Jockey Club who had once used the services of a top-notch local private investigator. His name was Michael R. Wysocki, and he specialized in criminal matters.

CHAPTER SIX

THE PRIVATE EYE

Mike Wysocki might have walked out of a movie screen during a scene depicting a private detective. He wasn't a fictional Sam Spade or Mr. North, but he looked a lot like a private eye was expected to look, and he talked and acted like one. He was of medium build, had dark hair that was rapidly receding, and was a cautious man who tended to carefully study the lay of the land and consider all the alternative moves and possible repercussions before making professional decisions.

He was the real McCoy—a former Las Vegas cop who'd worked with the Metro PD for six years in the Patrol Division and as an undercover narcotics officer, before leaving to go into business as a private investigator, a PI. A brother was still serving with the Metro PD, but Mike had a yen to dig into mysteries on his own to find out what was going on, and to tie all the strings together. There was a big demand, by private citizens and by attorneys with clients involved in criminal matters, for his services, and for the professional help of other properly licensed and experienced civilian gumshoes in Las Vegas.

When the Whites called on Wysocki for help, he was one of more than 140 private investigators licensed to practice in Nevada, and most of them worked in or near Las Vegas. State certification was a demanding process, designed to weed out and discourage dilettantes and amateurs. Each candidate for a license was required to pass a written examination and have at least 10,000 hours' experience as an investigator before being accepted. There's plenty for them to do, especially in Las Vegas, but it's not because local police don't work hard and do a good job.

The Las Vegas Metropolitan PD, which was formed in 1978 after the Nevada State Legislature approved merger of the city police with the Clark County Sheriff's Department, is professional and generally efficient. But like many police departments around the country, there is simply too much crime for them to deal with, and officers assigned to investigate homicide and other criminal cases are overworked. By necessity, tough priorities have to be established, and that can make it difficult for investigators to focus their efforts exclusively on a single case—especially when it isn't officially classified as a homicide or some other high-profile crime.

Even known homicides don't always get the attention many families and other survivors would like. Clark County has about one million permanent residents, and annually attracts another 28 to 30 million tourists. Las Vegas Metro is the primary law enforcement agency serving most of the area, employing about 1,350 uniformed officers to do the job. During 1995, the year before Bruce vanished, Clark County, including the city, recorded 154 homicides. During the early months of 1996, the year that he was reported missing, the comparative homicide rate was running far ahead of that.

Only fourteen homicide detectives were assigned by Las Vegas Metro to handle all those murders, as well as taking care of other responsibilities. Homicide investigators, who work in seven two-detective teams that vary in individual makeup from case to case, and sometimes from week to week, also probe suicides and every shooting involving a police officer. Las Vegas homicide detectives each investigate approximately twenty cases every year, about four times the workload of their fellow officers in New York, and twice the number in Los Angeles.

Some families of homicide victims, or other people who have been the target of major crimes, hire outside help to move investigations along if they can afford it. The Whites could afford it. The fees agreed to between the Whites and Wysocki were not discussed publicly, but the going rate in southern Nevada usually ranged between $75 and $100 an hour.

The private eye had already been in the business for seventeen years, and about 95 percent of his work involved investigation of criminal matters. Most of his clients were lawyers. So when the Whites telephoned him Sunday morning, he wasn't immediately sure he even wanted to take the job. They agreed on a meeting at the Whites' home later that day.

Anyone who is or has been involved in a big bookmaking business could be expected to have certain secrets to hide, but the Whites and Steve Weinstein assured the sleuth that they would give him complete cooperation. If he thought they had information he needed, all he had to do was ask, and he would get a frank and honest answer. No one in or outside the family would be off-limits to him, and they agreed to provide him with complete access to their personal affairs. They promised him *carte blanche* to do whatever needed to be done to find Bruce—or his body.

Wysocki agreed to accept the job, after advising the family that for the time being he didn't want them to tell anyone else about his involvement. It was a completely open investigation. Robin Loehr and her older sister, Shelley Faigenblat, weren't even to know about the agreement until he gave the okay. Amy also wasn't to know, until he decided it was time. Initially, Fred, Sylvia, and Steven were the only ones aware of the investigation. Brian Foster was the next to be let in on the secret, then Yohan Lowie.

The same afternoon that Wysocki agreed to take the job, he drove to the Castle Vista Estates to poke around and to talk with Lowie. The Whites had given the investigator the gate access code and he let himself inside. Lowie's Suburban wasn't in the driveway, so Wysocki called him on a cellular phone and the builder agreed to meet him at the Lowie home in a few minutes. While the detective was at Lowie's house, he noticed Amy standing on the second-floor balcony of Bruce's home directly across the street, watching him. The Whites had given him her photograph, so he recognized her.

When Lowie arrived, the two men went inside his home to talk and a few minutes later Wysocki noticed through the windows in the entranceway that a two-tone light brown work van had pulled up and parked in front of the Weinstein house. A short time later the driver of the van rang Lowie's doorbell. The man, who appeared to be in his late fifties, was there to clean Lowie's carpets.

Wysocki decided to interview Amy while Lowie was getting his carpets cleaned, and telephoned Mrs. White to ask her to call and let Bruce's girlfriend know that he had been retained to investigate the disappearance and wanted to talk with her. Then he walked across the street and rang the doorbell. Amy answered immediately and told him she had already talked with Bruce's mother, so she was waiting for him. Then she offered him a glass of water. As they walked into the kitchen, Wysocki glanced toward a table and saw one of the biggest syringes he had ever seen in his life. As a former undercover narcotics officer, he had seen a lot of them. The syringe on the table appeared to have a four- to six-inch barrel, and Wysocki cracked a little joke about drugs. Amy wasn't put off a bit.

She explained that she was a professional carpet cleaner, and that the syringe was used to inject fluid into carpets to get rid of especially troublesome stains. She'd used it to clean a piece of carpeting where Bruce's little girl had spilled some juice, Amy said.

Amy was chatty and friendly, and put her hand on the detective's arm as they walked into the kitchen. During the early minutes of their conversation, she busied herself fixing sandwiches for her carpet cleaner's two grandsons, who were waiting at the house with her while he was busy across the street at the Lowie home.

She seemed to be surprisingly relaxed and untroubled while Wysocki explained that the family had hired him to find Bruce and asked her what had happened at the house on Friday. Amy told him that he was free to look anywhere he wished, inside or outside the house. When he said he wanted to determine who her boyfriend had talked with recently, and asked for a copy of the bills for all the phones that Bruce had had access to in the house—including her celluar phone—she readily agreed to obtain them for him.

Amy didn't show any signs of the stress that a woman would normally be expected to experience if her boyfriend had just disappeared under such ominously mysterious circumstances. The Whites and Steven Weinstein were devastated, and expecting the worst. But their apprehension didn't appear to be shared by their son's girlfriend.

Amy told the detective that she had returned to the house on Friday at about 5 p.m. A short time later a man and woman who worked for Bruce had stopped to pick up some money he owed them. He'd led them into Kenny Reisch's office to take care of their business, and while they were walking through the laundry room leading into the garage, Bruce thought he smelled gas.

Bruce left with the visitors after finishing up their business, and drove to the Boardwalk Casino to spend an hour or so betting on horse races at the sports book. After he left, she telephoned the gas company and asked someone to have a technician sent to the house to check for a leak. A repairman showed up a few minutes later and, after carefully checking for trouble, told her he couldn't find any evidence of leaks. He suggested that the odor may have come from gas in one of the cars. Despite Bruce's attention to security, Amy opened up all the doors and windows to the house.

Continuing her account, Amy said that a friend of Bruce's had dropped him off back at the house early in the evening, and that he had been in a good mood. While he went to his upstairs office to take care of some business on the telephone, she fixed ravioli. When the meal was ready, she took his plate upstairs and offered to give him a massage if he was in the mood.

Everything about the evening was normal, until about 11 p.m., when she went into the bathroom to take a shower. She told Wysocki that she had already soaped her hair and body when Bruce opened the shower door and said he was going out. He was dressed in a clean T-shirt and shorts, and his long hair was pulled neatly back and tied in a ponytail. When Wysocki interrupted to ask for a more detailed description of the clothes Bruce was wearing, Amy said that the T-shirt was white with a V-neck, and she thought the shorts were black. He was also wearing black sandals.

Amy was surprised to see him out of bed and dressed, with his hair combed. Like everyone else who had had anything to do with Bruce, she knew he wasn't a night owl. His days were for business, and night was for sleeping. According to the story she told Wysocki, she quickly wiped off as much soap as she could and, still wet, stepped from the shower to follow him and ask what was going on. "I got some business to take care of. I'm going out," he said.

"When are you going to come back?" she asked.

"Well, I'm going to be back when I'm back," he replied. "If I'm not back by Sunday, take my kid and meet me up in Lake Tahoe." When Bruce walked out of the room, went downstairs, and left the house, it was the last time Amy saw him, she claimed.

The investigator had been in the house about a half-hour when the carpet cleaner came in and told Amy that he'd had to postpone the job at Lowie's home because the equipment didn't work. Amy introduced her employee as Bobby Jones, and told him who Wysocki was and what he was doing. Then she and Jones moved a few feet away and had a brief conversation before he told his grandsons that they were leaving and walked out the door.

While Wysocki continued to question Amy, they strolled through the house. The investigator walked along hallways and peered through rooms. He looked in the master bedroom, and inspected the spacious walk-in closet. Bruce wasn't the kind of man who carelessly peeled off a shirt, pants or shoes and dumped them on the furniture or floor. He was meticulously neat, and believed in the old saying: "A place for everything, and everything in its place." He had about twenty pairs of shoes, each pair in its proper place in a shoe rack or on the floor, where the overflow was lined up in careful order. There were no spaces in the rack or on the floor that would indicate that any of the footwear was missing.

About 4 o'clock Saturday morning, Amy said, she began calling hotels to see if Bruce was registered. By 5 o'clock she was telephoning hospitals. None of the hotels had a record of him registering as a guest, and none of the hospitals had treated or admitted a patient named Bruce Weinstein. Amy said that, after telephoning the hospitals, she went to Smith's Food King to get something to eat. At 7 a.m., Kenny Reisch arrived at the house to pick Bruce up and go with him to meet someone.

It was a strange story, and Wysocki was an experienced, alert investigator who had heard lots of stories and listened carefully for inconsistencies, miscues, and subtle nuances that could sometimes tell him as much about the narrator as about the yarn she was spinning. He was disturbed at Amy's habit of referring to Bruce in the past tense, using phrases like, "Bruce used to . . ." as if he was dead.

After they'd talked for about an hour and a half, Amy told him she thought her missing boyfriend was dead. She had accepted the fact that he wasn't coming back, and didn't know what to do. Feeling sorry for herself, she lamented that she had put everything into her relationship with Bruce, and now it was gone. She would have to get on with her life, and take care of herself. She told Wysocki that she thought her boyfriend may have gotten himself in trouble through some kind of drug deal.

While Wysocki poked through the house, she continued to trail after him, repeating her tale of woe. She never left his side. If he bent over to peer at shoes in a closet, she hovered over him. When he walked into an office, a bedroom, or into the garage to look through Bruce's car, she was right behind him. Before Wysocki had ended his look-around and conversation with her, Amy had become so fidgety that he suspected she had to go to the bathroom, but didn't want him out of her sight and on his own inside the house for even a few minutes.

At last, Amy told Wysocki that she had work to do, and he left. The PI hadn't found any suspicious physical evidence, or if he had, he wasn't saying anything about it. The search didn't turn up any traces of blood inside the house or immediately outside, and there were no signs of illegal drugs. It seemed that Amy was a good housekeeper. The interior of the home was neatly kept and meticulously clean. About the only thing out of place were some of the corners on the carpeting, that looked as if they were out of alignment or pulled away from the tack strips and turned up.

Before telling the story to Wysocki, Amy had tried it out on at least one other person, Shawn Hallman, and she still didn't have all the details down pat. Amy contacted Bruce's former brother-in-law and said she wanted to talk to him, so he went to the house on the Monday morning after the disappearance. The first thing she said when she met him at the front door was that she didn't want to talk to him inside the house because it might be bugged with audio or video recording devices. So she led him through the house and out the back door.

Amy was very mysterious, and not her usual self. She was normally self-possessed, and always meticulously groomed, but that morning she was a bundle of nerves and looked like she hadn't slept for days. She had no makeup on and was wearing a white bathrobe and carrying a plate with her breakfast—a little dry rice pancake. She told her puzzled guest that she was nervous, couldn't eat, and didn't feel good.

When Hallman asked what was wrong, she launched

into the story about Bruce interrupting her while she was in the shower late Friday night and telling her that he had to go someplace. Amy said she'd hurried from the shower, still soaped up, and ran after him, telling him to wait and she would drive him wherever he was going. But Bruce refused her offer and told her that if he didn't get home in time, Amy should go ahead to Lake Tahoe with Jaclyn and he would join them there.

Amy also complained that she was "cash-poor" and was stuck with about $15,000 in bills, including a huge phone bill from Bruce's gambling activities. Hallman advised her to search the house, because Bruce always stashed money around, but she replied that she was afraid to do that because cameras might record her activities. Then she asked the young man for a disturbing favor.

She wondered if he would help her out by testifying that Bruce had a lot of enemies—hardnosed characters who were likely to kill someone if they were crossed. Amy had seemingly come up with the idea out of nowhere. Hallman was shocked. He didn't understand why Amy would need him to testify about something like murderous enemies if Bruce was merely missing. That was the first time he had heard anything about a possible murder.

"Shawn, you know I would never do anything like this," she said. Her shaky denial was as upsetting as the talk of testifying about deadly enemies. Shawn hadn't accused her of murdering his former brother-in-law, and so far as he knew, neither had anyone else. He thought the whole conversation was bizarre. As he was leaving the house, Amy listed her phone numbers on a business card and said she wanted him to get back in touch with her. He never talked to her again, and left Las Vegas that day to drive back to his parents' home in California. He also ripped up the business card.

When Wysocki left Amy after their first meeting, he walked behind the house and climbed over a tall fence separating the development from a broad expanse of desert. He looked around for about two hours, searching for a body, clothing, or anything else that might provide a clue to the fate of the missing man. There were no fresh tire tracks or shoe prints, and no signs of blood. The area immediately behind the house had recently been cleaned and graded, so tracks would have been easy to spot. Wysocki also poked around houses in the development that were still under construction, looking under piles of boards and behind equipment, but found nothing suspicious.

In repeated conversations with Wysocki over the next few days, Amy's story changed in subtle ways. During their second discussion, when Amy recalled Bruce returning home Friday evening, she described him as being agitated, in a bad mood, and immediately going upstairs to his office and shutting the door. Other details also differed from the initial telling. One time she said that Bruce had handed his credit card to her before leaving, but in another version she said he'd left it on the credenza. She said once that when he left she watched from the top of the stairs, and in another version that she'd walked down as far as the L-shaped landing. Wysocki didn't miss any of the changes.

Later he continued his conversation with Lowie. The builder had some interesting things to say during the interview, and in subsequent conversations with other investigators. He told the detective that he had been in the house on Saturday and noticed an area of carpeting on the second floor just outside the master bedroom that appeared to have been recently cleaned. He also said that a few days before Bruce's disappearance, the rotund gambler had paid him for some additional work at the house with a couple of $5,000 chips from the Hilton Hotel and Casino. Lowie had seen him with the high-value chips before, but they had never been offered to him in payment for his work. Bruce thought nothing of walking around with his lone pair of scuffed sandals on his wide feet, a T-shirt pulled down over his expansive belly, and a pair of old tennis shorts, with $50,000 or so in cash and casino chips stuffed in the pockets. He kept the bills, most of them crisp new century notes, lumped together in a distinctive fold: After separating them into two neat, equal stacks of $500 each, he folded the end of one into the middle of the other, then pressed them together and wrapped them with a rubber band.

A week or two later, Lowie was working across town near the Hilton when he walked into the casino and tried to cash the chips. Casino officials didn't recognize him as one of their high-rollers, and when he was asked to talk to someone with more authority, he gave up on the project. It was too much hassle, so he returned the chips to Bruce and told him to pay him when he had cash. Bruce handed him $5,000, but he disappeared before he could pay off the rest of the money.

The already warm friendship between the home builder and the gambler deepened after Bruce moved in across the street. Bruce sometimes introduced Lowie to other people as his younger brother, and the builder accepted that as the compliment it was meant to be. Lowie was an industrious man, and he performed various odd jobs for his friend and for Amy when they wanted something special for the house.

Amy was constantly coming up with some project or other to make the house more livable and enjoyable. With Bruce's approval, she had had Lowie arrange for a crew to install marble on some table tops in the back yard. Lowie arranged for specialists to come in from California, and when they got there, Amy sent them away. "I don't need it right now," she told Lowie. "I'll call you when I'm ready."

That was the week before Bruce disappeared.

One day while Amy was busy on the ground floor, the two men slipped upstairs to the master bedroom closet and Lowie began to show Bruce how to operate the secret knob on the cabinet over the makeshift safe. The next thing they knew, Amy was peering over their shoulders. The empty compartment was open, and Bruce froze in his tracks. He didn't say anything. He didn't have to, because his chagrin was obvious. They had only lived in the house a few weeks and Amy already knew about the secret safe.

After his initial conversation with Amy, Wysocki still wanted to look around the house on Castle Vista Court on his own, without her dogging his heels. He also had a special project in mind that would be difficult to carry out if she was hovering over him, so he talked to Sylvia White and asked her to get Amy out of the house for a while. Mrs. White wasn't in a mood for dining out, but nevertheless she telephoned Amy and suggested that they get together for lunch. Amy said that her brother, Mickey Gerber, was flying into town from New Jersey at about midnight, to be with her during the ordeal over Bruce's disappearance, so Sylvia White invited him too.

Mrs. White's daughter Shelley Faigenblat and her husband had flown in for the mournful gathering of the clan—Robin had three young children to care for, but stayed in daily touch with the family by telephone. A party of five, Mrs. White, the Faigenblats, Amy, and her brother, eventually gathered around a table at the Cafe Nicole. Mrs. White, with help from her daughter and son-in-law, did her best to keep a conversation going as long as she could so that Wysocki would have plenty of time to check out the house, but it was difficult. They weren't in a chatty mood.

They managed to keep their side of the conversation going, although it was forced and strained.

Amy didn't talk much, but her brother talked enough for both of them. Mrs. White said he clowned around, and described Gerber's behavior during the meeting as particularly inappropriate. While Bruce's worried family members were forcing themselves to talk and to choke down their food, Amy's brother reputedly joked and laughed as if he didn't have a worry in the world.

But the awkward luncheon served its purpose and gave Wysocki time to go through the house in a search for the $5,000 casino chips that Lowie and members of Bruce's family had mentioned—and to carry out an experiment. The PI was intent on following up on unsettling reports by Lowie and Mrs. White of suspicious spots of moisture or signs of recent cleaning that they had noticed on the carpeting.

When the tenacious gumshoe let himself into the house with a key given to him by the Whites, he had a companion with him, a civilian forensics analyst with special expertise in the use of luminol. Little known outside of professional circles, it has been a part of the crime-fighting arsenal of detectives, evidence technicians, and laboratory analysts for decades. Luminol is an amazing chemical compound that makes it possible to detect the presence of blood invisible to the naked eye, even years after it has been spilled. It is so sensitive that it is capable of detecting a single drop of blood among 999,999 drops of water.

To be effective, it must be used in near-total darkness, and when blood is present the luminol will make it glow with a spooky blue-green light. The light is created when the chemical reacts with an enzyme found in the hemoglobin, the coloring matter in the red corpuscles of the blood.

If blood has been spilled, it will show up, even if the area has been scrubbed clean.

The luminol tests were a disappointment, and failed to turn up any tell-tale spots or other blood traces. The search for the casino chips also turned up negative. But the disappointment was only temporary, thanks to a colossal blunder by Amy.

She realized soon after arriving home from the luncheon that someone had been inside while she was gone. Upset, she telephoned Steven Weinstein at the Whites' home and told him about her discovery. At about 7:30 or 8 p.m., Wysocki telephoned and confessed that he was the intruder and had been looking for blood. After speaking with Steven Weinstein about Amy's earlier call, he was expecting her to be angry.

"Well, I understand you were upset a while ago," he said.

Amy had changed her tune during the brief cooling-off period between calls, however. "I was," she said. "I'm not now." She was chatty and friendly, even after he told her: "I just came over. I took a forensics expert in and I went in to look at the blood on the floor, on the carpet." That didn't appear to shock her at all, and she immediately blurted out: "Oh, you must have found blood. There's a lot of blood on the carpet. We cleaned it up, but Bruce used to get fantastic bloody noses."

Continuing to chatter, she said that Bruce walked around holding a towel to his bloody nose, and he bled so bad she had to use bleach on the towels to get the stains out. Blood got all over the floor.

Amy's statement was an amazing development, and a serious blunder on her part, one of a series of mistakes that would cast doubt on her claims of innocence in the complex mystery surrounding Bruce's disappearance. The statement also provided the private eye with an unexpectedly attractive opening to develop more information. Wysocki asked Amy to show him the blood spots, and said he would also like her help setting up an interview with Bobby Jones and another man who worked for her as a part-time employee. Wysocki deliberately phrased his request so that it was impossible to miss the inference that he was referring to other bloodstains as well as evidence of nosebleeds.

Amy agreed to arrange for her employees to meet at the house with the detective at 5 p.m. the next day, Thursday. She also agreed to his request to look at bloodstains, remarking: "I'll show you which ones are from the bloody nose."

She must have belatedly realized that the more she talked, the deeper she dug herself into a hole. Her mistaken assumption that Wysocki had found blood, followed by the story she'd volunteered about the nosebleeds, had seriously shaken her composure. After hanging up the telephone, she packed her bags and left the luxury home she'd moved into with her rich boyfriend barely seven months earlier. At 4:30 Thursday morning, she checked into the Gold Coast Hotel & Casino on West Flamingo Road. It was one of her favorite casinos and she loved the annual July poker tournament—but she hadn't checked in to play cards.

About two hours before the scheduled 5 p.m. meeting at the house, Amy left a message on Wysocki's pager. It was brief and to the point. "I'm terrified, but not of you," she said. Amy cancelled the interviews and hung up. About ten minutes later, she called back and left a message on his beeper. She asked him to leave a number where he could be reached, and to give her a half-hour lead time. As soon as Wysocki played back the message, he posted his office number on the beeper.

At 4:30 Amy telephoned him at the office. She was agitated, at times speaking in excited, hurried gasps as if she were peeking over her shoulder and expecting to see a monster sneaking up behind her. During the afternoon conversation, and a follow-up call she made a few hours later, Amy said she was terrified because people were after her. When Wysocki asked what was going on, and pressed her for specifics about the people she was scared of, she told him she felt like she was trapped in a box canyon. "You're on one side, his family's on one side, his friends are on one side, but at the entrance to the canyon are some very, very bad people, and I'm completely terrified of them.

"I'm not even driving my car now because they had a tracking device on my car. They've been following me around," she blurted. "I've been using other people's cars and these people have been chasing me around all day." She told the detective that her Camaro was in the parking lot at the Stardust and asked him to check it out for her. She wanted to know if it was bugged.

Wysocki agreed to take a look. He was intent on keeping Amy as cooperative as possible for as long as possible. He assured her that he would use the new information and help find Bruce's killers. If she knew anything, she should share it with him, he urged. When Amy suggested that Bruce may have been involved in a drug deal, Wysocki asked for names. She didn't have any.

Now the detective was trying to convince the agitated woman on the other end of the telephone line that they should get together, so they could sit down face to face and try to sort things out. Amy didn't fall for that, and continued to refuse to tell the detective where she was, or to meet with him. She was so frightened that she was going to change her identity and leave the country. She said she had already checked out extradition treaties, and knew which countries would send fugitives back to the United States.

Switching rapidly back and forth from apparent suspicion to talking as if Wysocki was her protector, the fidgety, flighty woman sometimes sounded like she thought he was working for her instead of the Whites. She asked if he knew where she could obtain false passports and other ID that she could use to change her identity. He was a private detective, and she figured he should know about things like that. Wysocki wasn't in the business of passing on that kind of information to other people, especially someone like Amy DeChant, who was acting increasingly like she had something terrible to hide. Something like involvement in a murder.

Early Friday, Amy placed another call to Wysocki to check up on his inspection of her car, and to open an intriguing new window that was either designed to shine new light on the investigation or to further obscure things. Although Wysocki drove to the Stardust to see if Amy's car was parked there, he didn't bother to look for tracking devices. But when she asked if he'd looked it over, he said he had and there was nothing there. Then he asked her for an honest answer to a query of his own that had been a long time coming:

"Amy, I got one question for you," he said. "Did you kill him?"

"There were four guys that did it," she blurted.

Amy admitted to Wysocki that the fanciful yarn about Bruce suddenly walking out of the house and promising to meet in Lake Tahoe was fantasy, a chimera designed to distract and confound. It was a cover story she'd concocted because she had been threatened and was scared to death. Bruce didn't leave the house on his own; he was taken away by mobsters, she said.

The alarming new version of the last night she spent with Bruce painted a far different scenario from the earlier account. Like the other story Amy had told the PI, the new tale differed in various details during its retellings to Wysocki and others.

The first time she recounted it to Wysocki, she said that four men barged into the house, and while one of them took her into a bedroom, blindfolded her, and tied her up, the others forced Bruce upstairs. Amy said her captor was armed with a big gun. While she was being guarded by one of the thugs, she could hear Bruce being beaten upstairs. Then she heard some shots, and Bruce's body was dragged or pushed downstairs and out the door. A few minutes later, one or more of the men walked into the bedroom, untied her, and announced that they were allowing her to live.

In another version, she related that she was taking a shower upstairs at about 10 o'clock Friday night when she heard a knock on the door. Moments later, a rough man who looked like a Mafia type suddenly appeared, dragged her out of the shower, and tied a blindfold around her eyes. Then he led her downstairs, and made her sit on the toilet stool in the bathroom. Her captor stayed with her, telling her he couldn't understand why a woman like her was involved with a man like Bruce.

While the thug was saying nasty things about Bruce, the frightened woman could hear the sound of a struggle upstairs. Then, with her eyes still shrouded by the blindfold, she heard three gunshots. A few moments later, she heard someone else enter the bathroom and announce in a harsh voice that the job was done.

It was an appalling story that created pathetic visions of a tiny, helpless woman perched on the toilet stool, blindfolded and faced by brutal, blood-thirsty killers. Amy was naked and defenseless, at their mercy, and waiting for a bullet to crash through her skull at any moment. But they didn't shoot her.

The single constant, every time she told the story to Wysocki and to others, was the reason she wasn't murdered with her boyfriend. She said the sinister gangsters told her, "The Mob does not kill women and children." Therefore, if she cleaned up the blood and kept her mouth shut, they would let her live. The intruders warned that they would be watching her, and she would be killed if she didn't comply with their demands.

Wysocki had listened to other hair-raising accounts by frightened or desperate people during his near quarter of a century as a cop and PI, and Amy's yarn was about as hard to swallow as it could be. He had peered under enough rocks while helping clean up some of the maggots and rot that infested Sin City to know that the Mob, Mafia, or whatever name was used for organized crime, simply didn't send out hitmen who worked like that. Stories about gentlemanly professional racketeers who spared women and children were bad fiction. The truth was that anyone who was a witness to a felony and could create a potential problem for the killers would be eliminated without a second thought. If women and children could be witnesses, women and children could die alongside the men.

When Amy repeated the more dramatic, lethal version of the yarn, Wysocki listened intently, occasionally asking for clarification of some point, or clearing up an inconsistency. When he asked her to describe the killers, she replied that she only saw one of them. He was an older man, wore a mask, and had a New York accent, she said. Amy pointed out that she was certain it was not a New Jersey accent, which is similar, because she was from the Garden State and familiar with the subtle differences in the speech of people who grew up in the adjoining states.

Wysocki asked if the intruders could have touched and left fingerprints on anything in the house that she didn't clean up, and she told him they were wearing gloves. What kind of gloves? he asked. "Work gloves," she said. "They were all wearing work gloves."

When Wysocki turned to the subject of clothes, she said she only saw the man who was guarding her, and he was wearing black pants, a dark jacket and a mask. It was a medium-weight jacket, like someone would wear to a ball-game. Wysocki suggested that might be overly warm for someone to be wearing on July 5 in southern Nevada, and Amy said she thought the jackets were probably part of a deliberate act to prevent her from identifying their regular clothes.

Wysocki noticed that early in the conversation, Amy's speech was seemingly spontaneous. But when he asked about things like the gloves and the jacket, she hesitated before replying, as if he had asked her questions she wasn't prepared to answer.

Amy's story about sinister Mob executioners who protected her from needless discomfort by taking care to tie her loosely, and commiserated with her about a nasty boy-friend, was hard to believe. The distraught woman claimed to be terrified of some kind of shadowy hitmen for organized gangsters, but he knew real professional Mob assassins don't take chances with witnesses. And they don't extradite people. Judicial authorities and government officials do that. The Mob doesn't extradite; it terminates.

At that point, no one, neither Wysocki, the Whites, nor police, had directly accused Bruce's girlfriend of deliberate involvement in his disappearance. But Amy knew she was suspected of killing him. In a brief conversation with Sylvia White shortly after the awkward luncheon, Amy told her: "I didn't kill your son. I loved your son."

"You have a sweetheart in jail," Sylvia responded. "How can you say such a thing?"

The reference to Amy's former drug-running boyfriend imprisoned in California made it obvious that some of her most closely guarded secrets were being dug up and revealed. There could no longer be trust between them. Amy and Sylvia would never talk to each other again.

CHAPTER SEVEN

BOBBY

The day after Amy fled the house on Castle Vista Court, Robert Wayne Jones stuffed a couple of fresh T-shirts, some underwear, and a few other personal items in a paper bag and went on the lam.

Pressure had been steadily building on the fifty-seven-year-old carpet cleaner ever since his boss's rich boyfriend disappeared and people began asking questions about what had happened to him, where he might be, and whether or not Bobby Jones had any of the answers. Amy was beginning to show serious signs of stress, and so was he.

Jones had been learning the hard way that getting close to Amy DeChant was like being a fly venturing onto a spider's web. Every step you took, and every tiny twitch of your body tangled you deeper and more securely in the spider's sticky trap.

Bobby wasn't a person who was comfortable with cops, or ex-cops who had become private investigators, and his unexpected brush with Wysocki at Amy's house was unsettling, although he had handled it well enough. The carpet cleaner was even more seriously shaken by a confrontation with Sergeant Larry Hanna, of the Las Vegas Metro's Missing Persons Division.

On Friday, less than a week after Hanna had taken the missing persons report filed by Steve Weinstein and Amy DeChant, the police sergeant received a telephone call from Mike Wysocki. Wysocki offered to share any information he acquired with police, and brought Hanna up-to-date on his investigation, providing him with names and telephone numbers. One of the names Wysocki passed on to him was that of Bobby Jones.

Hanna telephoned Bobby at his home and arranged for a meeting so they could talk. Bobby said he had to drive his two grandsons to the Roy Martin Middle School for a swimming class, and suggested they meet there.

Bobby was a loving, attentive grandfather who enjoyed the little boys and took them for rides in his car and in Amy's van. The day after Bruce vanished, he drove them into the desert to look among the scraggly yucca trees and the dry sandy soil for rocks for a landscaping project. They didn't come home with any rocks, but the youngsters were pleased with the outing anyway. They always had a good time with their grandpa.

When he had been lucky at poker or had more than his usual meager amount of cash, he was generous with the boys, and with his longtime wife, Cheryl Keyser. According to a witness, several days after Bruce disappeared, Bobby pulled out a wad of currency almost two inches thick, peeled off a pile of bills, and gave them to Cheryl.

Alan Bady, an occasional boyfriend of Cheryl's grown daughter, Suzanne Kathleen Anton, watched the whole thing, and later recalled that it looked like all the bills were C-notes. He figured there was at least $10,000 in the roll, which was folded over. According to Bady, Bobby got a little upset because his wife promptly telephoned her family in California, invited them to town, put them up at the El Cortez Hotel on Fremont street, and fed them dinner for three or four nights. Then she took him, Suzanne, a daughter-in-law, and the grandkids over to the MGM Grand Hotel and sprang for most of the costs for the party. Suzanne cashed her welfare check and helped pay for some of the festivities. They went on rides, ate ice cream, gambled, drank, and did whatever they wished.

At the Martin Middle School, Hanna was flagged down by a man driving a compact white four-door with two children in the back seat. After the boys left for their class in the school building, Hanna began asking Bobby questions about his association with Amy DeChant and Bruce Weinstein. Bobby said he had worked part-time for Amy for about four months, cleaning carpets and doing odd jobs at some of the properties she owned around town.

According to the story that developed during the conversation, Amy had called Bobby to the house on Castle Vista Court to clean up a couple of spots left on the carpet when Bruce's daughter spilled lemonade. One of the stains was upstairs, the other downstairs. He told the officer that he hadn't noticed anything unusual in the house. Amy had told him on Saturday that her boyfriend had disappeared, but didn't go into any elaborate detail about the mystery, he said.

When Hanna mentioned that Bruce's family thought he'd been killed, and asked if the carpet stains might have been caused by blood instead of lemonade, Bobby said he didn't think so. But some strange things had been going on, and Bobby told the investigator that Amy had telephoned him a couple of days earlier and asked him to leave the company mini-van in the McDonald's parking lot by the Stardust on the Strip so she could pick it up later. Bobby said he left the van as instructed, with a door unlocked and the keys hidden inside.

Hanna didn't like the smell of things, and his previous suspicions were intensified by his talk with the carpet cleaner. After leaving Bobby outside the school, the investigator drove back to his office, and telephoned the Homicide Division. Homicide detectives told him that they had already talked with Wysocki and knew about the missing bookie. They were on the case.

Las Vegas was quickly becoming too hot for Bobby, and after the disturbing conversation with Hanna, he telephoned his friend, Richard Reyes, and said he needed a ride. Reyes was another big man, a solid six-footer who was three inches taller than Bruce and kept his weight around 300 pounds. Friends sometimes called him "Fat Richie." Bobby's friend hadn't achieved the missing bookie's wealth or success, but he shared his passion for gambling, especially sports betting.

Reyes hadn't worked for a year or so, and spent much of his time in his two-bedroom house parked in front of a television set watching professional sports, checking out the lines and placing bets with sports books at different casinos around town. Mostly he stayed home with a succession of roommates he took in to help pay the rent, and when Jones phoned, he was doing what he usually did on summer evenings: watching a baseball game on TV. It was about 5:30 or 6 o'clock Friday night.

Bobby said that he was at the Hilton Hotel and Casino and asked Fat Richie to pick him up. The Hilton was just around the corner from Reyes's home, and he tossed on a clean T-shirt and a pair of shorts, jammed $6 into one of the pockets, and left the house to pick up his friend. Bobby was waiting when he pulled up. He had a pouch like those that dealers wear strapped around his waist, and was carrying a brown paper bag that was wrinkled and dirty. "What's up? Do you want to go to my aunt's, or your house?" the driver asked. "Kingman," Bobby replied.

Reyes had been expecting to chauffeur his friend a few blocks, and was surprised that Bobby wanted him to drive all the way to Kingman, Arizona. Bobby wanted to board a bus there for New Mexico. Richie asked if he could go back home and change out of his shorts, but Bobby told him he was in a hurry and wanted to start the trip immediately. "I want to leave until it blows over," he said.

Reyes asked his friend what he meant by "blows over," but Bobby wasn't in a mood to explain right away. "Well, I . . . the less you know, the better you're off," he said. Reyes changed the subject—slightly: "Well, what have you been doing all day?" he asked.

Bobby was fidgety, and stammered, "I, I've taken three buses, two cabs. I, I have detectives outside my door that were, you know, I said, I dodged them." He repeated the statement about the buses and cabs, and added that he also went to three different casinos. "I think I've probably lost them," he said.

Bobby was determined to get out of town as soon as possible. He could have taken a Greyhound bus, but that would have meant waiting until 12:30 the next afternoon, and he wanted to leave immediately. Reyes agreed to take him to Arizona, even though he was worried about whether or not his 1983 Lincoln Town Car would hold up on the three-hour round trip through the desert. It was primarily used to get around the city, and he didn't trust it on a long journey.

The two men were old friends who had met eight or nine years earlier when Reyes worked with Bobby's son, also called Bobby, at the Vegas World. Most people who knew both the father and son called the younger man Bobby Junior, to avoid confusion, but he wasn't really a junior. The middle names of the father and son were different, and the younger man's full name was Robert Raymond Jones. Almost everyone, however, family, friends, and fellow employees, knew both of them as Bobby Jones.

Amy had also worked with Reyes and the younger Bobby at the Vegas World while she was dealing poker there. Like Reyes, she got to know the older man through his son. Las Vegas is a big city, but for the people who float from job to job in the gaming business, it's a small world. They work together, they gamble together, and sometimes they get into trouble together.

Reyes and the elder Jones sometimes played poker together. The older man was a fixer and a tinkerer and he also took care of most of the mechanical problems with his friends' cars. Whenever Fat Richie's car developed a troublesome new rattle or clink that threatened to cause a breakdown, Bobby popped open the hood or crawled underneath and made the repairs. He also serviced the car, greasing it and changing the oil, so he was familiar with it and knew how it ran. Reyes trusted his judgment.

After climbing into the Lincoln beside his friend, Bobby assured Reyes that the old clunker would survive the trip, and promised that if there was any trouble, he would take care of it. He also said they could stop along the way to fill the tank, check the oil and water, and put air in the tires. Bobby promised to pay for everything. They stopped at the first Rebel station they saw to take care of the car, bought some bottled water and Diet Pepsi, then steered for Arizona.

They were barely on their way before they had to switch drivers. The rattletrap Lincoln had a muffler problem, and when there was too much weight in the front seat it sometimes dragged along the surface of the streets. Bobby couldn't match Reyes for size, but he weighed between 180 and 190 pounds. With approximately 500 pounds in the front seat, they didn't get very far before the muffler started to scrape. They didn't have anything to tie it to, so they had to exchange seats. The muffler still scraped, so they switched again, and Fat Richie wound up back where he started—driving. The muffler was still bouncing around underneath.

While Reyes drove, Bobby began to chatter. The older man was nervous, and clearly shaken up. He told his friend that he had to get out of town because of a child support problem with his ex-wife. Bobby said a detective who'd questioned him had taken down the numbers on his driver's license, vehicle registration, and Social Security card, and he was afraid police would put two and two together and pick him up. He said he had already been picked up once for non-support and had to put up $500 to stay out of jail— and the cost doubles for the second offense. Bobby said he didn't have that kind of money. Reyes wasn't sure which he was talking about, bail or fines. But there was no question about the amount of money.

Fat Richie knew it was true that a man could create serious misery for himself over child support, but it must have seemed that police were thinking of investing a lot of manpower in running Bobby down for a civil offense while so many stick-up men, rapists, and cold-blooded killers were stalking the streets.

Bobby was taking the matter very seriously, and hinted at other problems he was worried about. The woman he worked for was in big trouble of some kind involving her rich boyfriend who was missing, he said. The runaway carpet cleaner was still stammering: "Amy is in trouble, right? Amy is in trouble. I don't know, I, I, don't want nothing to do with her. I, I, I, she, she, she, she must have told the police I had something to do with it. I had nothing to do with it. All I did was clean some carpet." He was babbling, and running off at the mouth like he couldn't stop. "You know what I mean? I had nothing to do with anything. But, uh, I, I've got to go. I have never been this afraid. You know what I mean?"

Reyes had never seen his friend so upset. If Bobby's story about the child support problems, and being pulled into his employer's troubles over her missing gambler boy-friend, was true, it was understandable that he would be concerned. But Bobby was an emotional mess, and the fear was obvious in his face and in his fractured, staccato speech.

Fat Richie wasn't one of Amy's friends or associates, but he knew who she was. He had seen her with Bobby and knew she was his boss in the carpet-cleaning business. He had been having some difficulties with her himself. For the past three or four days she had constantly telephoned his house, asking him to leave messages for Bobby. She called him during the day, and she woke him up at night, leaving numbers where Bobby could contact her. When Bobby didn't get in touch, she phoned Fat Richie back with a new message or a new number to call. Reyes began suspecting that his carpet-cleaning buddy was having some kind of romantic affair with his boss. He speculated that Amy may have called Bobby at his house once too often, and his wife was becoming suspicious.

Bobby had been trying hard to avoid Amy, but finally instructed his friend to tell her that he would meet her at the Star Casino in Albuquerque, New Mexico, at 5 o'clock on Wednesday. Reyes didn't think his friend was serious about the meeting, and asked him why he was sending her on a wild goose chase. "You're not really going to Albuquerque to meet this chick, are you?" he asked. "No, I just want her off my back," Bobby replied. "You know what I mean? I want, she's crazy, you know?"

When Reyes and his passenger reached Kingman, they were greeted by a policeman, who pulled the car over and gave the driver a ticket for a missing taillight. Bobby sat beside Reyes while the ticket was being written out, with his mouth shut. After the policeman left, Bobby puttered around, making some minor repairs to the car.

The trip from Las Vegas had taken about twice as long as anticipated, and it was almost midnight when Reyes pulled the Lincoln up to the isolated little bus depot. There was only one bus, and a line of passengers waiting to board. The destination sign on the front said "New York." Bobby studied the schedule, and the news wasn't good. The next bus for New Mexico wasn't due to leave for six or seven hours, and in the meantime the depot would be closed. Reyes knew that his rumpled passenger had family or friends in the Baltimore area, and suggested that it might be a good idea to go there, but Bobby had his mind made up. He was going to New Mexico.

It looked like he had a long, lonely wait ahead of him, and the only retail business they could see within walking distance that was still open was a McDonald's. The men decided to drive to another restaurant to eat, and Bobby paid the bill. When they returned, the New York bus was still in front of the depot, and the dishevelled fugitive went inside to talk with the driver. He figured that if the bus was going to New York it would probably pass through New Mexico to get there and the driver could drop him off. The driver agreed, but before Bobby climbed aboard with his pitiful paper-bag luggage, he asked his friend to do one more favor. He gave Reyes $100 as expenses for the trip, and another $200 for him to give to Cheryl Keyser. The worried man tried to give his friend an additional $20 for gas, but Reyes figured Bobby was hurting for cash. He turned it down.

Bobby asked Reyes to call Cheryl at her job at a Las Vegas pawn shop, and tell her to be in the poker room of the Excalibur Hotel-Casino at 9 o'clock Tuesday morning when he would telephone and have her paged. He cautioned Reyes to be sure and contact her at work, because he was afraid to use his home phone.

Reyes had a lot of things to think about during his long, lonely drive back across the silent desert to Las Vegas. When he got home he relayed the message to his friend's wife, and Tuesday morning he picked her up at her home on 19th Street and drove her to the Excalibur. Cheryl had been Bobby Jones's wife for about twenty years and, like her husband, she was a regular around the poker tables in Las Vegas. For a while she'd worked as a floor supervisor at the Bourbon Street poker room, which was another of the favorite haunts of Bruce and Amy.

Reyes and his companion played a little poker while waiting for Bobby's call. He was twenty-five minutes late, and talked with his wife for fifteen or twenty minutes. After concluding the conversation, Cheryl told Reyes that her husband had promised to call her again about a week later, at 1 p.m. on a Wednesday at the Showboat Casino. Cheryl and Fat Richie showed up on schedule at the Showboat and played poker for two or three hours, but Bobby never called.

Reyes figured Bobby was hiding out at his son's home just outside Albuquerque. But when he called the younger man, Bobby Junior said his father wasn't there and had only telephoned him once after leaving Las Vegas. Bobby Junior was angling for a job at the Star Casino in New Mexico, but he was out of work and hanging around home by the time his father went on the run.

CHAPTER EIGHT

CAT AND MOUSE

The heat was on, and Las Vegas police and Wysocki had their hands on the controls, turning up the burner by the hour. Amy and Bobby were both on the run. No warrants were sworn out for either of them, so they weren't officially fugitives, but police were plainly as eager for face-to-face meetings as Wysocki was. Neither Amy nor Bobby wanted to talk.

Except for the fact that the harried grandfather and the manipulative, greed-driven woman were both on the lam, their reactions to their sudden illumination in the spotlight of a missing persons investigation were radically different.

Wherever Bobby was, he was cagey enough to keep his head down and his mouth closed. Based on statements he'd made to friends, he figured that if he could just stay out of sight and out of the clutches of the Las Vegas Metro police long enough, things would eventually blow over.

Amy reacted like a doe momentarily illuminated in a car's headlights. After a moment of frozen immobility, she exploded in sheer panic, first darting one way, then clatter-ing off in another direction. She was seriously spooked and behaving as if she really believed her own preposterous stories about sinister Mob assassins stalking her every move.

Although Amy had left the luxurious home once shared with Bruce for the last time, she was still hanging around Las Vegas, fluttering from here to there, and playing a frus-trating cat-and-mouse game with her pursuers. She used ex-boyfriends, employees and various other people she had been associated with to run errands, provide shelter, and front for her, or play the role of stand-in during contacts with the private detective and the police.

While Wysocki and police were fitting promising new pieces into the challenging jigsaw puzzle the investigation had developed into, and steadily ratcheting up the pressure on Amy, she was ranging all over Las Vegas. If she wasn't keeping the telephone lines quite as busy as Bruce's former bookie operation, she was doing her share to keep the Sprint telephone service financially healthy and in the black. She contacted old boyfriends, former employees Bobby Jones and Claudia McClure, Bobby's friend Fat Ri-chie Reyes, Mike Wysocki, and police, leaving names and numbers of cell phones, beepers and telephones at private homes, hotels and casinos.

Amy didn't check into the Gold Coast to rest or to play poker. One of the first things she did was begin contacting ex-sweethearts and asking for favors. She would be busy throughout the weekend, but she would have an especially hectic day and night on:

Thursday, July 11

She was already playing telephone tag with Wysocki when she called Keith Bower. Bower was still working at the Primadonna, but he was home when Amy telephoned at about 11 a.m., and told him she needed a place to stay for a while. She didn't say anything about being in trouble, and he told her to come on over. Amy replied that she was at the Gold Coast and needed to be picked up.

When Bower drove over Amy met him with several heavy suitcases and a couple of huge plastic garbage bags stuffed full of clothing, what appeared to be business files, and other items. She was agitated and while he was driving her to a Chinese restaurant on Spring Mountain Road for lunch, she blurted out that she was in trouble. Her rich boyfriend had been murdered and some people were looking for her. Amy said she was afraid she was going to be killed.

Instead of asking Bower to drive her to his house after lunch, she said she had to go to a couple of banks to draw advances on her credit cards. She said she was so scared that she was going to leave town, but she only had a couple of thousand dollars in cash, so she was going to get as much money as she could from her credit cards and also take her jewelry out of a safe deposit box. Amy had six or eight credit cards in her purse, and told Bower she also had a gun. He never saw a weapon and she didn't mention it again.

Bower drove his harried friend to the First Interstate Bank (FIB) at Eastern and Bonanza, then to another bank on Charleston that was later taken over by Wells Fargo. She told him that she got a $10,000 advance at the FIB, and $5,000 at the branch bank on Charleston. At one of the banks she apparently cleaned out a safe deposit box, but Bower never saw any jewelry because she was carrying a briefcase.

Amy was never known for talking much about her personal finances, but while Bower was driving her around Las

Vegas, she babbled about her money, Bruce's money, credit cards, jewelry, and lock boxes. She was feeding off her own excitement and fear, and the more she talked, the more wrapped up she got in telling the story. She acted like she couldn't stop herself.

Amy told her friend that Bruce had a half-million dollars hidden in the house. It was his working capital. But when she looked for it, she couldn't find it. He had another $6 million or $7 million stashed in safety deposit boxes at various hotel casinos around town, but she'd given the keys to those to Bruce's family, she said. Amy claimed she had to leave town with as much cash as she could put together because mobsters were looking for her, and her life was on the line. She invited Bower to go with her, but he refused.

While they were driving, Amy kept a nervous watch in the rearview mirror to see if anyone was tracking them. Bower didn't see any cars that appeared to be deliberately following. Amy acted so seriously spooked that he asked why she didn't go to the police for protection. If she wasn't involved in Bruce's murder, she should just ask law enforcement authorities for help, he reasoned. She told him she couldn't. If she went to the police, the assassins would eventually catch up to her and she wouldn't have a chance.

At last, Amy asked Bower to drop her off at the Palace Station so she could hire a cab. Since he wouldn't leave town with her, she had decided it was best if he didn't become any further involved in her troubles. Bower drove her to the Palace, helped unload her luggage, and went home by himself.

Robert Moon was still employed at the Las Vegas Hilton hotel and casino, and was working the 8 a.m. to 4 p.m. shift at the Island Bar when he heard from his onetime girlfriend. A voice mail message from Amy was waiting for him on his answering machine when he returned home at about 5 p.m.

She asked how he was doing, then volunteered in a pained little-girl voice that she wasn't doing very well. Amy left him a telephone number and a room number, asking him to call her back. Her voice sounded so tired and vulnerable, he worried that she might be in a hospital. Moon was surprised when he punched in the number and got the Stardust Resort and Casino. The desk clerk told him that no one was registered in the room. Amy didn't call back at his home number.

Friday July 12

Moon didn't hear from Amy until Friday when she telephoned the Hilton and talked with his bar manager. The manager told Moon that she had called and said she needed to talk to him because of an emergency. But she refused to identify the nature of the emergency or say where she was, and the manager told her that under those circumstances he couldn't ask the bartender to call her back. So Amy asked him to tell her friend that she would stop by at the bar later in the day.

It was about 2:30 p.m., near the end of the puzzled bartender's shift, before Amy showed up. She had a little bag not much larger than a purse that Moon later described as an "AWOL bag" slung over her shoulder by a strap. It was her only visible piece of luggage. The vibrant, enthusiastic woman whom Moon was used to had changed drastically. Amy was fidgety, and depressed, and looked as washed-out and rumpled as one of the towels she claimed to have laundered and bleached after Bruce's terrible nosebleeds. Amy said she needed a place to stay and asked if she could camp for a while at Moon's house.

She explained that she was having trouble with her boyfriend and needed a few days away from him, no longer than a week, to get her thoughts together. She didn't go into details about the nature of their problems, but Moon was understanding. He said she was welcome to stay, and gave her a key to the house. Amy needed another small favor. She asked the big man if he would mind picking her luggage up from the bell captain and taking the bags to her house when he got off his shift. He agreed.

The bartender was mildly surprised as he watched her leave. Instead of walking directly to the exit, she went all the way around the blackjack tables and vanished from his sight somewhere among the lights and slot machines. It was a circuitous route that might have been taken by a tourist or out-of-town gambler trying to find her way out of the casino. Amy was no tourist, and she knew her way around.

Moon experienced another mild surprise when he picked up the luggage. There were seven pieces, including two or three large suitcases, a couple of smaller bags, and a single huge plastic garbage bag that was packed full. They were all heavy.

Moon was already home and had fed his dogs when Amy knocked on the door at about 6 p.m. She had barely walked inside the house before she cleared up the minor mystery over her curious behavior when she took the long way out of the casino after their conversation earlier in the day. She asked her host if he had seen anyone following her when she left. He hadn't. The casino was busy, but people were occupied gambling or catering to gamblers, and there was no indication that anyone but Moon himself was paying special attention to her behavior.

Amy still looked untypically tired and wan, as she sat down to talk about her troubles. Her boyfriend was extremely jealous and looking for her, so she needed a place she could hide out while she tried to sort out her problems, she said. After they chatted for a few minutes, Moon took his skittish houseguest out to eat, then they stopped for a while at Danny's Slots. While they were at Danny's, she told him that she had a safe deposit box at the Stardust and asked him to drive her there so she could check it out. At the Stardust she scribbled her signature on a slip and Moon signed as a witness so the woman at the cage would allow access to the box, then stood a few feet away from her in a hallway while she took care of her business. He didn't see if she put anything inside or took anything out. During a telephone conversation several days later, she told him that she was going to give him a key to the lock box because she wanted him to have access to it, but she never followed through.

Amy was clearly nervous. She looked behind her frequently, and acted as if she was convinced someone was following them. Moon didn't see any evidence of that, but Amy continued to fuss.

It was about 10:30 p.m. when they left the Stardust and Moon drove them back to his house. It had been a long day for Amy, but she still had work to do. She went into the guest room and began pulling things out of the garbage bag, unloading other luggage, and hanging up clothes. Amy left the door open, and when Moon walked past before going into his own room, he noticed that she was busy writing in a notebook. Amy said she was making some notes to help her get things clear in her mind. She didn't say what those things were.

After Amy dropped the bombshell story on Wysocki about the Mob doing away with her boyfriend, the private sleuth telephoned the police department and said he had important new information involving the Bruce Weinstein investigation. Detectives assigned to the case were off duty, so a couple of general detail investigators and a sergeant drove out to the Boulder Highway to meet with the PI. He brought them up-to-date, and they ultimately passed the data back on to homicide investigators.

At the suggestion of police, Wysocki met with homicide detectives at Bruce's house, and arranged with the family to provide a consent to search. With the signed consent in hand, detectives Jimmy Vaccaro and Phil Ramos went directly upstairs to the master bedroom. Amy had told Wysocki to check the bed because it was bloody. The police officers flipped over the mattress, and were confronted with a broad welter of bloodstains spread over the mattress and box-spring.

Immediately, the police investigators left the house and contacted their superiors at the Homicide division, advising that they needed a search warrant. When it was obtained a short time later, Homicide investigators Paul Bigham and Thomas D. Thowsen, along with crime-scene analysts Michael Perkins and Bradley Grover, joined the other detectives in the search for evidence. Wysocki, who wasn't covered by the terms of the search warrant, wasn't included among the team of investigators who re-entered the house. A quixotic peculiarity of the law enforcement system favors private detectives by allowing them more leeway in some activities than police. Although a private investigator could look around the house with no more than an informal okay from a resident or family member, police were required to play by different rules. Once Wysocki began working hand-in-hand with police, however, some of the same rules that applied to them began to apply to him.

The search included a new round of luminal tests in the master bedroom, the small upstairs family room, the hallway just outside, and on the stairway. This time the evidence technicians had a better idea than Wysocki's expert of exactly where to look, they had different chemicals, and as much time as they needed. They waited until it was dark outside before they sprayed suspected blood-spot areas—and hit the jackpot.

The chemical illuminated a broad blue circle roughly one-and-one-half to two feet in diameter. A luminescent trail of blue led from the spot out of the bedroom, through the family room, into the hall, down the stairs, and outside the front door. The trail was intermittent, and a spot near the bedroom door and a couple of others on the stairs were much broader and heavier than the rest. After nearly a decade of experience, about half of it with Las Vegas Metro, Perkins thought the eerie glowing trail of blue resembled drag marks more than the results of a heavy drip or flow of blood.

Detective Thowsen agreed. "You could see exactly, you could see the railing and the steps and all this blue blotchy stuff all over from where the body was thumping down the stairs," he later recalled. "It gave a real tale as to what happened." The crime-scene analysts took pictures of the blue glow patterns, opening the camera lens wide for thirty seconds or more to compensate for the darkness.

The criminalists also conducted a painstaking search of the house for the large amount of cash that Bruce was said to have kept on hand. All they found was about seven dollars in coins scattered at the bottom of the hole-in-the-wall. The cabinet had been moved and the safe was wide open and exposed when investigators walked into the closet. The search failed to turn up any owe sheets from the bookie operation.

The investigators also failed to find any empty bullet casings, or any bullet holes in the walls or furnishings. The presence of bullet marks can be an indication of a sudden or unplanned shooting. In that kind of shooting, several shots are often sprayed around a victim, some of them striking home and others going astray. Planned shootings involving killers who have figured out what they're going to do ahead of time are less likely to result in superfluous bullet holes in the surrounding area.

Earlier that Friday afternoon while police were processing Bruce's house for evidence, Amy telephoned Wysocki. Unaware of the new search, she told the PI that she was trying to work out a problem. She'd left some of her personal business records at the house, and wanted to give them to a woman who worked for her. But Amy was afraid to go back.

"I'll tell you what," Wysocki offered. "After 8 or 9 o'clock I'll go to the house, if you trust me." Amy responded that she didn't trust anybody.

"If you trust me, I'll get the records and I'll bring them to you," the PI persisted. Amy agreed, and told him where they were. Then they set up a meeting at the Stardust, so he could hand them over to her in the parking lot. Amy said she would park her Camaro on the north side of the lot and meet him there at 3 p.m. next to the car.

Wysocki telephoned the Homicide Division and told officers about the latest development. Sergeant Ken Hefner relayed the information to detectives Bigham and Thowsen, who were still at Bruce's house.

Bigham is a big bear of a man with a mop of curly black hair, and a natural gregariousness that on the surface might seem to clash with the role he has to play as a Metro police detective assigned to investigate grisly murders and suicides. He is not one of those hardened, weary, veteran investigators who have been drained of emotion and burned out by too much blood, too much misery, and too much horror. He has the air of someone who enjoys life, and his love for his work is obvious. When he talks about a promising break in an investigation or closing in on a killer, he is energetic and animated. The words rush out in an excited tumble and he uses his hands and arms.

Like quite a few of the men who wound up with the Metro police, Bigham was brought to Las Vegas through his service with the United States Air Force and a duty assignment at Nellis Air Force Base just outside the northeastern edge of the city. He was sworn in as a police recruit in the morning and discharged from the Air Force in the afternoon. He went right into the Police Academy with no time off. Thowsen was one of his instructors.

More low-key than his sometime partner, Thowsen was already a near-twenty-year veteran with the department when he was assigned to the Weinstein case. Like Bigham, the Air Force brought him to Las Vegas. Thowsen grew up in an Air Force family. Following a tour of duty in Germany, his father was assigned to Nellis and retired there. Thowsen spent his high school years in Las Vegas and remained in the city as an adult.

After completing his academy training, he started off as a patrolman riding in a black-and-white, as other Las Vegas police officers do. Then he moved into the K-9 Unit, and worked for four years with a Rottweiler named Bosco as a partner. After Bosco developed cancer, Thowsen was assigned to the Police Academy as an instructor and eventually moved into the Detective Bureau before joining the Homicide Unit in 1992.

His sandy hair and light complexion give him a physical resemblance to Missouri Congressman Richard A. Gephardt. Thowsen tends to get a bit rumpled toward the end of the day, but he is thoughtful and quick to smile. Smiling is something he does when he is talking about a successful investigation and getting the goods on a bad guy or gal and putting them out of circulation.

The two detectives had assumed the role as case officers,

or primary investigators, by the time they were notified of the meeting Wysocki set up with Amy, and Bigham told the PI he would meet him at the parking lot.

The private detective was waiting in his car with the files stuffed in a big bag when Bigham showed up. Although the parking lot was jammed with cars and people, the homicide detective spotted the Camaro with the tell-tale vanity plate as soon as he arrived. The men talked for a couple of minutes. They agreed that Bigham would walk a few yards away until he saw a woman approach Wysocki. Bigham was dressed casually. He blended in. If everything went as planned, Amy would walk into an ambush and find herself face to face with a homicide detective whether she liked it or not.

A few minutes after Bigham set up his surveillance, a car stopped a few feet away, a woman got out, approached Wysocki, and started to talk. Bigham pounced. As the startled woman turned to see who the newcomer was, the detective introduced himself. "Hi," he said. "I'm Paul Bigham."

The woman responded by introducing herself. She was Claudia McClure. "Get in my car," Bigham commanded, while grabbing her by the arm. "We're gonna have a chat."

Responding to one of the first of a barrage of questions from the exasperated detective, the woman said she wasn't sure where Amy was.

"Why are you here?" Bigham demanded.

"She [Amy] was afraid this would happen," Claudia responded. Amy didn't want to make the pickup herself because she suspected police would be waiting for her. So Claudia hitched a ride with a male friend, who agreed to drop her off at the parking lot and was waiting in his car.

In many ways, Claudia McClure was typical of people who hung around the casinos—and around Amy. She played poker, Bigham learned after questioning her, and worked as a sometime shill, sitting down at the tables to keep games going so that other gamblers would stop to play.

Bigham and Thowsen weren't gamblers and weren't especially knowledgeable about the activity, but it seemed that half the people they talked to while investigating the Weinstein case were poker players.

"Everybody played poker," Bigham said. "Both Bobby Joneses—father and son, Cheryl Keyser, Claudia McClure, Amy, Bruce . . . With some it was a demanding hobby; with others an obsession."

"These guys will go and work an entire shift, like at the Rio, dealing poker, then they'll get off shift and go to Palace Station and play poker for six hours trying to win some money," Thowsen marveled. It's common for obsessive poker players to work six months or a year, he said, save as much as they can, then quit and play poker until their cash runs out. Then they start the process all over again.

Claudia McClure also worked hard at other jobs outside the casinos, and had become one of Amy's most dependable employees. She cleaned airplane interiors for Amy and also had several houses that she regularly cleaned on her own. She told Bigham that when she'd returned home after completing a job, a call from Amy was on her voice mail. Amy wouldn't tell her where she was, but asked her to pick up the Camaro and some records from a private detective at the Stardust. Bigham arranged to have the Camaro impounded, and it was hauled away from the Stardust until a search warrant could be obtained and detectives and crime-scene analysts had a chance to go over it thoroughly.

But Amy herself was proving to be a slippery quarry, who was as elusive and hard to pin down as ectoplasm; she was a phantom voice on the telephone that never quite materialized into solid flesh. Wysocki and police knew she was still carrying on her helter-skelter ramble through Las Vegas, but trying to toss a net over her was about as difficult as filling an inside straight—it was something clearly within the realm of possibility, but tough to do.

Amy wasn't dealing any more with Missing Persons, but she continued to initiate calls and to return calls to homicide detectives, through she wouldn't agree to a face-to-face meeting so they could take a formal statement.

Shortly after the ambush misfired at the Stardust, Amy agreed to talk with homicide investigator Jimmy Vaccaro if Wysocki could be included in a three-way telephone conversation. Vaccaro called Wysocki, who drove to the homicide office to wait for Amy's call. When she called, the trio talked for a while on the speaker phone before Amy said that she wanted to speak privately with Wysocki. The PI was still doing his best to keep their contacts friendly, and listened patiently while Amy ran through a shopper's list of grievances and troubles on a separate line.

"I don't know why they want to talk to me. I don't know why they're pushing me," she said. The private eye and the homicide cop both told her the same thing: she should come in to the office for an interview. Amy still wasn't ready to do that. "I don't know why they want to talk to me. I don't know why they're pushing me," she pleaded with Wysocki during the private chat. Wysocki couldn't talk her into coming into the Homicide Division offices, and neither could Vaccaro, although both tried their best. All that the effort accomplished for Vaccaro was a spot on Amy's "nasties list" alongside Sergeant Hanna.

After Wysocki's frustrating exercise in three-way verbal fencing, Amy telephoned him at about 11 p.m. and complained that she was mad at Vaccaro because he had pressured her when she wasn't ready to talk to him yet. What really got under her skin was a statement he'd made about her "accomplices," she said, looking for sympathy from the private eye. "What do you mean by accomplices?" she claimed to have shot back.

Wysocki told her that he didn't know for sure what Vaccaro had meant, but assumed it was a reference to Bruce being killed in the master bedroom, then carried downstairs. The bookie weighed close to 300 pounds. "Look at you, you're a little thing," the private detective reminded her. "What?" she demanded. "They think I couldn't move him by myself?"

If Wysocki's remark had seriously bruised her ego, the damage was only temporary. Amy continued to phone him. He realized that she was a woman who revelled in her ability to manipulate and control men. Wysocki played along and managed to stay in her good graces. He allowed her to believe that she was pulling his strings, while he used the opportunity to keep track of what she was thinking, and doing and tried to figure out exactly where she was.

Detectives Ramos, Bigham and Vaccaro had all attempted to get Amy to talk after the investigation of Bruce's disappearance was officially moved from Missing Persons to the Homicide Division. Despite hours of frustrating negotiations over the telephone, no one had had any luck in getting her to come into the unit headquarters for an interview.

Earlier in the investigation, as the murder probe was just getting underway, Sergeant Hanna tried unsuccessfully to get her to consent to a sit-down talk. She spilled out the same dubious story that she'd told Wysocki about Mafia hitmen killing Bruce in the bedroom. After returning a call left by the persistent police department sleuth on her pager, Amy tried to provide some cover for Bobby Jones, and said that when he cleaned the carpet he didn't know what had occurred in the house. In response to a question, Amy said she'd picked the van up after Bobby dropped it off, but couldn't remember where she'd left it. She sounded frazzled and flighty, and Hanna couldn't get her to agree to talk face to face with him. So he suggested she might be more comfortable talking with Vaccaro.

Amy said she was too frightened to come in and talk to either of them, and was convinced her vehicles were bugged with tracking devices. She had to have time for rest, she said, to get control of herself and possibly talk with an attorney before she would be ready to consider an interview with police. She terminated the call after leaving a voice-mail number with Hanna. After she hung up the telephone, Hanna dialed Homicide to relay the information to Vaccaro. Other officers there told him that Vaccaro was already at the apparent crime scene at 5452 Castle Vista Court. The homicide detail was officially taking over the investigation.

Like the hummingbirds that fluttered from one hardy desert bloom to another, pausing just long enough on the prickly pears, saguaro and brittlebush to suck out as much of the juices and pollen as possible before moving on to the next, Amy was constantly on the move, and never settled down anywhere.

Saturday July 13
Saturday morning Amy told her host she had found another place to stay and would probably be leaving later that day. Moon was off work for the weekend and was planning to help a friend shop for a pickup truck, but Amy asked him to do another favor for her before she left. She said her work utility van was in the parking lot at the Boulder Station and asked him to pick it up for her and drive it to the house. She explained that she didn't want to go with

him because she was going to take a shower and get ready to leave.

Moon agreed to pick up the van, and she told him the key was inside, under the driver's side floor mat. Amy had once cleaned his carpeting so he was familiar with the vehicle, and he knew she didn't have a car with her. He drove to the hotel and casino on Boulder Highway with his friend, then drove the old Ford Aerostar back to the house. His friend drove Moon's car back.

Amy was inside the house when they got there, so Moon parked the van in the driveway and left with his friend. Moon's own pick-up was being serviced at a Pep Boys and he needed to pick it up before 4 p.m. When he finally completed his chores and returned once more to his home, another heavyset man he had never seen before was helping Amy load her luggage into a small white stationwagon parked in the driveway. She introduced the newcomer as a trusted friend and said his name was David. The big man had dark hair and beard. Before leaving, Amy told Moon that he would be receiving a telephone call from Metro police that had something to do with her rich boyfriend. The boyfriend's name was Weinstein, she said. That was the first time Moon had heard Bruce's name, but it wouldn't be the last.

Moon didn't see David again, but over the next few days he accepted some telephone messages from him and relayed them to Amy at another number.

Sergeant Ken Hefner had been a cop nearly seventeen years, having worked the robbery detail before moving into homicide. As he walked into his office on Saturday morning, another officer told him Amy had called, and he realized he had a golden opportunity. Amy had asked to talk to either Detective Vaccaro or to Detective Bigham. Neither of the investigators were in the office, so Hefner took the initiative and punched in her voice mail number. He waited an hour, and when she hadn't returned the call, he telephoned her again. This time she immediately called back, and he told her it was very important that she come into the homicide unit headquarters for an interview to help investigators figure out what had happened to Bruce, already missing for more than a week.

Amy was nervous and apprehensive. She said she was scared to come in because she was afraid she would be arrested. She repeated the fear four or five times, and Hefner reassured her that no one was planning to arrest her. They had no cause to, and merely wanted to take a statement. Finally, he convinced her. Amy told him that she had a couple of errands to run first, and would come in to Homicide for an interview at 1 p.m.

The astonishingly inventive and elusive woman was unaware that while she was talking with Sergeant Hefner, Wysocki was parked outside the house she was calling from. The private eye had used caller ID to trace an earlier call from her, and set up surveillance at the house. When he got to the home he saw the brown cleaning van in the driveway, and after he spotted Amy, he telephoned Homicide and talked with Hefner. Hefner was already talking by phone with Amy when Wysocki called. The experienced police sergeant did a first-rate job juggling the calls, and while he was keeping Amy on the line, he dispatched the two case detectives to join the private eye outside the house.

The homicide officers pulled their cars up beside Wysocki's just as Amy was leaving with David Ward, who rented an older house she owned downtown and was a personal friend. Unaware they were being watched, the man and woman climbed into the work van and drove it along busy Charleston Boulevard. Bigham, Thowsen, and Wysocki were all driving separate cars, and with the two city police detectives maintaining contact with Hefner by telephone, they set up a rolling surveillance on the van.

Rolling surveillance is difficult under the best of circumstances, and traffic was heavy. The three investigators lost the van after tracking it for a mile or so along Charleston Boulevard. Apparently unaware they were being followed, Amy and her companion dropped the van off at the parking lot of the Macayo Restaurant at the corner of Charleston and Bruce and left in another vehicle.

A couple of minutes after 1 p.m., the slippery, fast-moving woman who had led investigators on such a bizarrely erratic chase, knocked timidly on the front door of the Homicide Unit office.

While Sergeant Hefner led the fidgety woman inside, she told him she was afraid she was going to be arrested. He repeated his assurances that she had nothing to fear, and introduced her to the detectives who would take her statement. By that time, Bigham had become the lead investigator, and Thowsen was assigned as his partner on the case, so they conducted the interview. Hefner didn't sit in on the talk.

Amy had been on the run for three days, and the emotional wear and tear was obvious. She was dressed casually in shorts and a top, and despite her studied effort at vivaciousness, the worry and the pressure of shuttling from friend to friend, house to house, and casino to bank while switching from car to van to taxi, showed in her face. She looked tired, but seemed determined to put on her best performance. She was chatty, warm and coyly feminine. She also worked to give the detectives the impression that she was a vulnerable woman targeted by the unfair suspicions of police, and forced to go on the run from more sinister elements because she feared for her life.

But she didn't behave like she was struggling with dreadful emotional trauma, like many people the experienced detectives were used to talking with during investigations. Amy especially didn't strike them as a woman who was so recently put through the trauma of practically witnessing the brutal murder of her boyfriend by a gang of hired assassins. She alternated between chatty, perky and friendly, to frightened and fragile. She frequently got up from her chair to pace around the small room, and was obviously rehearsed and prepared, but her story was preposterous.

During the entire ninety-minute interrogation, conducted at a long, straight table in a spartanly furnished room, she consistently peered at cryptic notes scrawled this way and that on a piece of paper ripped from a composition book. Some of the notes were scribbled horizontally, others climbed the sides of the sheet in steep vertical lines, and still others slanted across the page or were squeezed in an even more scattershot manner. One of the officers would ask a question, and Amy would peer down at the paper, then turn it like it was a wheel until she found the answer she was looking for. It was a bizarre performance, and one that was filled with glaring holes and inconsistencies.

Amy repeated her story about the Mafia-like characters invading the house and taking Bruce away, but like other tellings, some details were either left out, added, or embellished. In the version recounted to Bigham and Thowsen, she said that she was taking a shower when a rough-looking man barged inside, dragged her out and began hustling her downstairs. At the top of the stairs she looked down and saw Bruce's silhouette outside through a big picture window at the entrance to the house. The figure was flanked by the dark shadows of two or three other people, but she was able to distinguish her boyfriend's silhouette by his size, and by the long ponytail that dangled over his shoulders.

Bruce was marched upstairs after she was moved into the bathroom of the guest bedroom, blindfolded with a scarf or towel, told to keep quiet, and made to sit on the stool while one of the intruders stood guard. While she sat alone with the thug, and Bruce was brought inside and marched upstairs, her guard asked why she was hanging around with scum like the big bookie. She said she heard the sound of an argument, fighting, and a series of gunshots. A few moments later, she said, a different man came downstairs and warned her to keep her mouth shut about the violence she had just witnessed.

"We're not going to hurt you. We don't hurt women and children. But we know who you are. We know who Bruce's child is, and where to get ahold of you guys," she quoted the thug. Then the newcomer advised that there was a mess upstairs, and ordered her to clean it and get rid of everything. "We'll be watching you, and we'll know if you call the police," he added.

When Amy recounted the remark about sparing women and children, Bigham and Thowsen glanced at each other, and rolled back their eyes in disbelief.

Continuing her statement, Amy said she waited a while before leaving the bathroom, then walked upstairs and started cleaning up. She said she worked all night, taking only a few short breaks. When the bedroom and surrounding areas were finally in order, she gathered up all the rags and other cleaning material, stuffed it into a couple of small trash bags and loaded them into her car. Then she drove around the neighborhood and tossed the bags into trash cans or Dumpsters at banks and retail stores.

Bigham later poked through a couple of Dumpsters behind stores and banks that Amy had mentioned, but didn't find anything helpful to the investigation. Bruce had already been missing for more than a week, and the trash bins had been emptied at least once during that period.

During the lengthy interrogation, Amy added a few other variations to previous run-throughs of the story, including the disclosure that when she went into the garage she realized some large remnants of excess carpeting stored there were missing. The inference was obvious: Bruce's body was wrapped in the left-over carpeting and taken somewhere to be disposed of.

Amy told the interrogators that Bruce was involved in various shady dealings in addition to his bookmaking activities. He had used drugs in the past, and made deadly enemies during some of his shadowy adventures, she claimed. While it was true that Bruce had experienced some drug problems several years earlier in California, he had put that behind him and everyone—except Amy—whom police or private investigators talked to insisted that he was dead-set against narcotics. He didn't use them himself, he wouldn't hire anyone who used them, and he didn't want anything to do with anyone who might be involved in the abuse of or trafficking of drugs.

The interrogators had other reasons to believe that Amy was spinning a web of lies, cleverly attempting to mix a minimum of fact with a maximum of fiction. One of the reasons involved a story told by Yohan Lowie. Chance observations by the peripatetic home builder on the Friday night she claimed Bruce was murdered by mobsters made her account almost impossible to believe.

Lowie hadn't yet installed an electric meter to automatically turn on water sprinklers in the community, and he left his home at about 10 p.m. to manually water lots he had already landscaped so he wouldn't lose the grass and plants to the devastating south Nevada heat. He was walking a short distance from his house and heading toward the gate a few minutes after 10 p.m. when he heard three popping noises that were spaced about five or ten seconds apart.

The sound seemed to have come from behind him and Lowie turned and looked toward the Weinstein home, which was only about 200 yards down the street. It was a light, windy night. The street was well illuminated, and Bruce had paid for extra lighting, so the front entrance was plainly visible. Lowie didn't see anyone outside.

He noticed the garage doors standing open and Amy's Camaro parked outside at the side of the curb. Bruce's Lincoln was parked inside in its usual place, but normally at that time of night, both cars were in the garage and the doors were closed. Lowie was vaguely disturbed because Bruce was extremely security conscious and careful to make sure that all the doors and windows in the house, including the garage, were locked at night.

It was the night after Independence Day, and Lowie mentally wrote off the noises as nothing more significant than kids playing with left-over firecrackers.

After watering the front lawns, Lowie irrigated the back yards, before finally calling it a night and returning home at about 11 p.m. Amy's Camaro was still parked on the street, and Bruce's Lincoln was still in the garage with the bay door closed. The home builder had worked outside for an hour or more and hadn't seen anyone enter or leave the Weinstein residence, or anyone come through the security gates. There were no screams or any other unusual sounds, except for the popping noises. It wouldn't be very long before Lowie would have good reason to question his assumption that kids were merely playing with firecrackers, and wonder if there was a more sinister cause for the noise.

Amy's story didn't compute when she told it, and it

didn't match well with the accounts of Lowie and other people whom the detectives, their colleagues and Wysocki had already talked with. Bigham and Thowsen gave Amy a couple of rest breaks during the lengthy interview and she took the opportunity to walk around outside.

Wysocki had shown up and was talking with colleagues of Bigham and Thowsen outside the headquarters when Amy told him that she needed to settle down. She needed a hug! That touch was pure Amy. When she got into trouble, she would grin or hang her head and tell the nearest man that she needed a hug. Wysocki was the nearest man, or the most convenient.

After returning to the interrogation room, about an hour into the interview, she started to cry, stood up and went into her "poor little Amy" mode. She tearfully advised the startled detectives: "I need a hug!" This had never happened before in an interrogation conducted by either of the officers, and the situation wasn't covered during their police academy training. They were embarrassed, but they were anxious to keep Amy friendly and in a talking mood. Awkwardly, one at a time, with their backsides jutting out behind them so there would be as little body contact as possible, they leaned forward and gave the sniffling woman cautious arms-to-shoulder hugs. "It was the kind of hug someone gives to their grandmother," Thowsen later recalled.

With that taken care of, the detectives decided it was time for a break so they could talk things over among themselves. While they compared impressions, Amy could sit in the room and stew. That technique had helped loosen up more than one suspect, who was playing fast and loose with the truth.

Bigham was married and the father of three girls, and his partner was married to a medical doctor and was the father of a daughter by an earlier marriage. They knew enough about the feminine psyche to recognize some of the games Amy was playing. When dealing with someone like her, subterfuge and lies were about as predictable as the hourly explosions from the pseudo-volcano on the Strip.

Despite Amy's carefully rehearsed testimony, the scribbled notes and the histrionics, the performance was unconvincing. It didn't jibe with the physical evidence, and statements from other people the investigators had talked to. Looking back later on the interrogation, Bigham observed: "Basically we got down to the point where we didn't believe a damned thing she said. You know, she was fabricating a lot of it."

Amy was still whimpering, huddling in her chair and looking tiny, fragile, and defenseless when they returned. The detectives didn't waste time, and told her they thought her story was pure hokum. There was never any Mob, and they believed she had more to do with Bruce's disappearance than she was telling them.

Amy's transformation was immediate and dramatic, like snapping off a switch. She stopped sniffling and sat up in the chair, crossing her legs and folding her arms protectively over her chest. The helpless, frightened demeanor she had previously shown vanished, her blue eyes narrowed aggressively, and her attitude turned icy cold.

"That's it," she snapped. "We're done."

The tape-recorded interview, which would eventually cover sixty-nine transcribed pages, was over. When Amy stalked out of the office she didn't look back, but her confrontation with one of the interrogators wasn't over. During a break, Sergeant Hefner had talked with Ward, who drove her to the homicide division offices. Hefner explained that the meeting was still going to take a while, and said he would see to it that Amy had transportation if Ward didn't want to wait around. The driver left.

Detective Thowsen was drafted to drive her back to town after the interview ended. Before sliding into the front seat of Thowsen's car, Amy exchanged a few words with Wysocki. She wasn't grinning, hanging her head or asking for a hug. She was in a dark, nasty mood and the verbal exchange with Wysocki was short. Amy wasn't her usual chatty self during the long drive with Thowsen, but she took the opportunity to try and worm some information out of him.

If he and his partner believed she was responsible for killing Bruce and were afraid she would run away, why didn't they arrest her? she asked. Thowsen thought fast and replied that they believed she was the kind of woman who would realize the trouble wasn't going to simply fade away, and she would want to face down her problems in order to bring things to a conclusion. The truth of the matter was that police couldn't arrest her because they didn't have a body. They couldn't conclusively prove that a murder had been committed; they couldn't arrest her because they couldn't prove Bruce was dead.

Amy snorted and half-chuckled. "Well, I'm not really worried about running away," she said. "I've already checked into the countries that I'd want to go to and they have extradition treaties anyway." Thowsen thought over the remark on his drive back to Homicide headquarters. Amy had obviously done her homework, and she was still toying with the investigators.

Although Amy quickly vanished again after she was dropped off by Thowson, the van was still at the Macayo and the police officers immediately arranged to have it seized, loaded onto a flatbed police trailer and transported to the impound lot. Amy had told them where she left it.

After the work van was impounded, evidence technicians processed it along with the Camaro, searching for clues to help solve the mystery of Bruce's disappearance. Perkins discovered a suspicious liquid in a cleaning machine inside the van, that appeared to be blood residue. A sample of the substance and a white towel with a blood-like stain on it, also recovered from the van, were carried to the police laboratory for more conclusive tests.

One of the more interesting items they found was a Jiffy Pop can with a false bottom that converted it into a handy mini-safe. Someone, presumably Amy, had stuffed a few hundred dollars in currency inside, along with two checks from the Aetna Bank. One of Amy's ex-boyfriends, who was apparently still carrying a torch for her, had signed the checks and told her to fill them in and cash them when she needed money. Bigham later interviewed the boyfriend, but didn't determine if they were the only signed checks the man had given her.

The search team also found a hanging badge-type of picture ID card in the van carrying the name of Michael A. Lucarelli. It was airline ID designed to permit Lucarelli to board and clean airplanes.

Sunday July 14

Amy telephoned Moon and asked if she could give his number to friends to relay messages to her. He said it was okay.

Police returned to Bruce's house a couple of nights after their initial search with crime scene analysts to carry out additional luminol tests, and to follow up on some other areas of the investigation. The house had already been released as a crime scene, and Bruce's family turned over temporary custody to Wysocki. All the locks were changed, and he had the keys and the security system code, so he let

Identification Report

Booking Number: <u>199800001118</u>

Last Name:	First Name:	Middle Name:
DECHANT	AMY	RICA

Alias:

Sex: Female
PIN Number: CJP: 1998-01-29 09:06:01
ORI Number: FL0560000

Birth Date: 3/19/48
Driver's License Number:
Birth Place: NEWARK, NJ
Address: TRANSIENT
Phone Number:

SSN:
Driver's License State:
Citizenship: US

Features:

Race: White	Weight: 120	Eye Wear:
Skin:	Hair Style:	Dental:
Build:	Eye Color: Blue	Facial Hair:
Height: 5'03"	Hair Color: Brown	Scars/Marks:

Employment Information:

Employer: Supervisor:
Occupation:
Address:
Phone Number:

Next of Kin Information:

Relationship:
Address:
Phone Number:

Arrest Information:

Arrest Date: 1/28/98	Booking Date: 1/29/98
FBI Number:	State ID Number:
OCA Number: 9800101144	ORI Number: FL0560000
Arrest Disposition:	Arrest Disposition Date:

Offense Details: NCIC Code: 9000 : 1/28/98
; 9000 : 1/28/98
:

Identification report prepared by St. Lucie County Sheriff's Department officers after the arrest of Amy DeChant in Port St. Lucie, Florida. (Courtesy St. Lucie County Sheriff's Department)

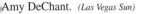

Amy DeChant. *(Las Vegas Sun)*

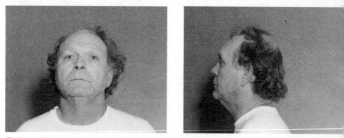

Robert Wayne "Bobby" Jones. Police mug shot taken after his arrest at his home in Las Vegas.
(Courtesy Las Vegas Metro Police)

The new, $675,000 Spanish–Style house on Castle Vista Court in Las Vegas occupied by Bruce Weinstein and his girlfriend, Amy DeChant, when he vanished.
(Courtesy Las Vegas Metro Police)

Blood stains, invisible to the naked eye, after they have been illuminated by the chemical Luminol. They show the path taken when the body of Bruce Weinstein was dragged or rolled down the stairs of his home. (Courtesy Las Vegas Metro Police)

Hole in the wall of Bruce Weinstein's master bedroom closet used to hide a stash of currency and casino chips—believed to have amounted to $100,000 or more—that helped finance his high-stakes gambling. (Courtesy Las Vegas Metro Police)

Bloody mattress in the master bedroom at 5452 Castle Vista Court in Las Vegas, where gambler and sports bookie Bruce Weinstein was shot to death.
(Courtesy Las Vegas Metro Police)

Blood stains on the foam sheet beneath the mattress Bruce Weinstein was lying on when he was shot to death.
(Courtesy Las Vegas Metro Police)

Gated and walled community on the southwest edge of Las Vegas where Amy DeChant and Bruce Weinstein lived before his mysterious disappearance.
(Courtesy Las Vegas Metro Police)

The shallow grave where the remains known as Old Alamo Road Doe were discovered. The slender man standing in the ravine at the upper left is one of the rabbit hunters who discovered the body. Las Vegas Metro Homicide Detective Thomas Thowsen is in the group standing along the upper lip of the ravine.
(Courtesy Las Vegas Metro Police)

Detective Paul Bigham of the Las Vegas Metro Police Department Homicide Unit, lead investigator in the Bruce Weinstein slaying.
(Photo by author)

Detective Thomas D. Thowsen of the Las Vegas Metro Police Department Homicide Unit. Detective Thowsen was a case agent working with Detective Paul Bigham on the investigation.
(Photo by author)

David J. J. Roger, Chief Deputy District Attorney who headed the prosecution of Amy DeChant and Robert Wayne "Bobby" Jones. Roger is at his desk at the Clark County Courthouse in downtown Las Vegas.
(Photo by author)

The Out of Bounds restaurant in south Florida where Amy DeChant trained as a bartender while she was living at a nudist camp, hiding out under the alias Sandy Wade.
(Photo by author)

Trio of St. Lucie County Sheriff's Department officers who collaborated in the apprehension of Amy DeChant after she was profiled on the television program, "America's Most Wanted." From left to right: Detective and lead investigator Charles Scavuzzo; Detective Derrick Peterson; Sergeant Diane M. Thompson of the Criminal Investigations Division.
(Photo by author)

officers inside and accompanied them during their second search.

The crime scene analysts cut out or pulled areas of the carpet away from the padding and wooden risers underneath to disclose a curious sticky substance that appeared to be blood. Samples were collected and sent to the police laboratory for testing by trained serologists to determine if it was blood.

Monday July 15

On Monday, ten days after the bookie vanished from his home, Amy telephoned Keith Bower to tell him that she was okay, still frightened, but alive. Regardless of what he might hear, she wanted him to know that she didn't kill Bruce, she said. Before hanging up the telephone, she told him to watch the 6 o'clock news. She was going to be on television. That night and the next morning, stories appeared on television and in the *Las Vegas SUN and the Las Vegas Review-Journal* about the police investigation into Bruce's disappearance. Hefner told reporters, "Foul play is suspected."

Police had issued a press release about the investigation, and it shook some interesting fruit from the tree.

Thursday July 18

On Thursday Bigham was contacted by a woman who said she had an audio tape that he should listen to. She had read a newspaper story about the investigation and recognized the names of Bruce Weinstein and Amy DeChant. The caller explained that she wanted to stay anonymous and wasn't ready to come in to the homicide unit headquarters to give a statement, but the tape involved several telephone conversations between Amy DeChant and Michael Lucarelli. Lucarelli was the husband of her friend,

Katherine Sue Gallagher, who secretly taped his conversations because she suspected he and Amy were carrying on an affair.

The conversations weren't part of a back-alley romance. They were about the suggested shakedown of a big-time Las Vegas bookie named Bruce Weinstein. When the suspicious wife listened to the tapes, they scared her so badly that she gave them to her girlfriend to keep for her, along with a handful of hastily scribbled notes.

The tapes disclosed that Amy and her former live-in boyfriend had discussed various schemes to hornswoggle Bruce out of a big chunk of his money. Lucarelli was a former reserve police officer in Henderson, a town of about 25,000 people on the southeast outskirts of Las Vegas, and he still had his badge. He figured he might be able to squeeze a juicy payoff out of the big-time bookie by flashing his badge, staging a phony arrest and threatening to see that he was put in prison if he didn't cooperate in the shakedown scheme.

They also talked about the possibility of bringing a few roughnecks in on the caper and extorting money from Bruce by pushing him around or threatening violence. None of the suggestions were very sophisticated, and there wasn't much likelihood they would have worked on a man with Bruce's street smarts and knowledge of the way real police actually worked. But they were discussed, and the discussions were on tape.

At that point the only thing Bigham knew about Lucarelli was that he'd apparently once cleaned airplanes for Amy. The husky homicide sleuth was intrigued, but his tipster was gun shy and seemed to be wavering over exactly how closely she wanted to become involved in the increasingly complicated investigation. The detective urged her to come in to talk and to bring the tape with her, but she begged off. She needed more time. Bigham told her to think things over carefully and to keep in touch. If she wasn't involved in Bruce's disappearance, she had nothing to fear.

The woman wasn't involved, but she was afraid anyway. If she turned over the tape and gave a statement, it would be easy for Lucarelli to figure out where the leak was, she told Bigham. For the time being, the matter was put on hold while the detective followed up other leads.

The efforts of investigators were given a major boost when Bruce's family announced a $50,000 reward for information leading to the recovery of his body, and for the arrest of his killer or killers. The reward was set up to be split down the middle, with $25,000 earmarked for help recovering the body, and $25,000 for the arrest. Tips should be phoned in to the Secret Witness program or to detectives attached to the Metro police Homicide Unit, it was added.

News accounts carrying the reward offer said police were continuing to look for fifty-seven-year-old Robert Wayne Jones, who was wanted for questioning in the case. Police had evidence that Jones had been in Weinstein's house shortly after he disappeared, the stories related. Bruce was described in the stories as a professional gambler. It was a description he had always preferred over his other business calling as a bookie.

When the reward was announced, people started telephoning Fat Richie, interrupting him while he was watching sports on TV, and suggesting that if he knew where Bobby was hiding out, they could go to the authorities together and collect a juicy reward. Reyes told everyone basically the same thing. Lots of people, including Bobby's family, wanted to know where he was. Even he didn't know where his friend was, and the callers were too late.

Several weeks passed before the tipster who had contacted Bigham about the Lucarelli connection called him back and said she was ready to come into the homicide division offices for a talk. She was spooked when her friend Katherine telephoned and said she wanted the tapes back. Christine Annette Johnson, a thirty-six-year-old Henderson woman, told the homicide investigator she was concerned because Katherine told Lucarelli about the tapes.

After taking the statement from Johnson, Bigham called Lucarelli into the headquarters and gave him a chance to tell his story. In the taped statement the mortified car sales-man admitted that he did have the conversations with Amy, but wasn't involved in Bruce's murder. Bigham believed he was telling the truth, so a once-promising suspect was quickly erased from consideration. Nevertheless, the detec-tive now knew of the shakedown discussion with Amy, and he had one more building block for his case.

The net was tightening.

CHAPTER NINE

AMY ON THE RUN

Sergeant Douglas Verzi was driving to work to begin his 3 p.m.–to–1 a.m. shift with the Harford County Sheriff's Department in northeast Maryland when he turned off of High Point Road onto State Route 23 and fell in behind a maroon 1993 Pontiac Bonneville with New Jersey license plates.

Although he was wearing his uniform, Verzi was in an unmarked patrol car. The driver of the eastbound Bonneville obviously didn't realize who was behind her because she was barreling along the isolated country road at about thirty miles over the speed limit. She didn't slow down after the other car pulled in behind her.

Verzi paced her for about one mile, clocking the Bonneville at 85 miles per hour, then activated the flashing lights on the police car. The driver of the out-of-state vehicle immediately slowed and pulled over to the right-hand shoulder of the road next to a cornfield.

The veteran county sheriff's deputy had just begun his

shift a half-hour early—and he was going to be working late.

It was almost exactly 2:30 p.m., Wednesday, July 24, 1996, and the speeder he'd pulled over was Amy Rica DeChant. Bruce Weinstein had been missing less than three weeks, and the woman suspected by Las Vegas police of being involved in his presumed murder had traveled 2,000 miles from home.

The diminutive motorist was the only occupant of the car and she was already holding her license in her hand when the deputy walked up to the driver's-side window. She handed the document to him before he was able to say anything. Then she reached down and hiked her skirt up over her legs so that he could see the white crotch of her underwear. It was a move that was blatant, implicit with sexual promise, and impossible to miss.

Verzi focused his eyes on the driver's license. It had been issued in Nevada, but the woman, who continued to sit quietly with her skirt hiked up, was driving a car with New Jersey plates. The deputy asked if she lived in Nevada, and how she happened to be driving a vehicle registered in New Jersey. She'd borrowed the car from a friend in New Jersey, and lived in Nevada at the address on the license, the driver replied. The address listed a post office box in Las Vegas. When Verzi asked what she was doing in Maryland, she said she was sight-seeing.

Advising her to wait in her car, the officer returned to his car and ran a routine motor vehicle check with the state of Nevada, which confirmed that the woman had a valid driver's license. He ran another check with the FBI National Crime Information Center.[1] The NCIC computer en-

[1] In 1999 the FBI unveiled an upgraded NCIC 2000 computer system head-quartered in Clarksburg, West Virginia, that does all the old tasks of its

abled a police officer to learn almost instantaneously if a particular car had been reported stolen, or an arrest warrant issued for the driver anywhere in the country. The check came back negative: the Pontiac wasn't stolen, and the flirtatious driver was not listed as wanted by any local, state or federal law enforcement agency.

The seasoned lawman also called the Sheriff's Department headquarters in the Harford county-seat town of Bel Air and asked for backup. The moment the woman in the Pontiac hiked her skirt up, he figured there was potential for serious trouble and he wanted to get other officers on the scene. He wasn't sure of her motivations for the brazen maneuver, but figured it was probably one of two things, neither of them good. Either she was setting him up for a later accusation of impropriety, or she was trying to divert his attention because she had something to hide—and that could be almost anything, including a gun.

Verzi had one more base to touch before writing out a speeding ticket. He asked for the car registration. While Amy rummaged through the glove compartment, Verzi peered into the car and noticed a photocopy of a map on the passenger seat, tracing a route from New Jersey to Baltimore. A big circle was drawn around a section of Baltimore that he recognized from his training in Narcotics as a tough, dangerous neighborhood notorious for cocaine dealing, where the dope trade was controlled by vicious street gangs known as Jamaican posses.

---

predecessor, in addition to offering vital new services to local, state and federal law enforcement agencies. In addition to providing lists of wanted persons, criminal histories, missing and deported people, and stolen firearms, vehicles, license plates, and other items, the new system offers automatic processing of fingerprints and mugshots. Law enforcement officers at a police station, jail, or in a squad car can place the index finger of a suspect into a tiny reader that transmits the unique print patterns by radio to the NCIC computers and conducts an instant check.

Amy couldn't find the registration, and finally gave him the car owner's insurance card. Verzi ran a check comparing the license plate with the name on the card, and everything matched. The same woman was named on all the pertinent documents.

Except for the skirt-hiking incident, which the deputy outwardly ignored, he seemed to have made a routine traffic stop, so he wrote out a speeding citation and handed the ticket to the driver. He told her why he had given her the ticket and was explaining that she could pay by mail or fight it in court, when she said she didn't have much money and asked if he could let her go with a warning. Verzi replied that it was too late for that. He had already written the ticket and there was nothing at that point he could do to change it.

During the entire confrontation, Amy tried to avoid looking at the police officer. She looked at the floor of the car, at the door, or at his belt buckle, but she wouldn't look at his face, and especially avoided looking him in the eye. She was a bundle of nerves. Her hands shook when she handed documents to him, and they shook when he gave them back. Even her arms quivered, and she behaved as if she was about to jump out of her skin.

Verzi was already suspicious that the fidgety woman with the hiked-up skirt had something to hide. The skirt incident, her excessive nervousness, the borrowed out-of-state car and the license with a post office box address were all unusual. But the seventeen-year law enforcement veteran had other, more compelling reasons for the nagging feeling that something was fishy.

The portion of Maryland Route 23 where he made the traffic stop was part of a notorious drug trafficking corridor, and narcotics enforcement was Verzi's primary area of expertise. For eleven years he'd worked as an undercover narcotics officer, and was in charge of the Sheriff's Department Drug Interdiction team for two years before recently transferring back to on-the-road work taking advantage of his specialty. It was his job to identify vehicles and drivers who might be transporting contraband narcotics through Maryland, and especially through Harford County.

At that time, Harford County was a narcotics transportion hot-spot, on a popular route from New Jersey, which had become a portal for importation of drugs into New York and other states. Interstate Highway 95 was the most direct route from New Jersey to the rich drug markets in Baltimore, Washington, Virginia and the Carolinas, but it was heavily patrolled by Maryland State Police. The area of Maryland that cut through rural Harford County a few miles north and west of the interstate had become a popular alternate for drug couriers who wished to avoid state police. The smart traffickers frequently used the less heavily patrolled back road between Delaware and their cut-off route to Baltimore.

The driver Verzi stopped along the rural state road was beginning to resemble profiles of drug couriers developed from personal experience by himself and other officers, as well as through formal studies of hundreds of arrests. The quality of performance, even the survival of officers like Verzi, can turn on instinct and knowledge gained through personal observation. But instinct and suspicion alone aren't good enough for the courts. After Amy signed the speeding ticket, Verzi had to tell her she was free to go. It was the law. Maryland criminal codes require police to advise motorists that they are free to leave after the initial matter they were stopped for is settled, even though the law enforcement officer may be getting ready to launch a drug interdiction investigation.

Although Amy was told she could drive away, she

elected to stay where she was and chat for a while with the policeman. Amy didn't know when to stop talking with a man, even if he was a law enforcement officer and she had something to hide.

Verzi told her that he worked for the drug interdiction team, and briefly explained his duties. Then he asked if she had any weapons, large amounts of money or drugs in the car. Amy hesitated for a few seconds before replying, "No."

Verzi's backup hadn't yet arrived, and the longer she remained parked beside the cornfield and in a cooperative mood, the better. It would give other officers time to show up. In the meantime, he went into his routine, asking questions and getting her to talk, while listening and watching carefully for inconsistencies, changes in replies, and excess jitters.

As Verzi continued to ply her with questions she became more antsy and distressed than ever. He asked where she was coming from, and she replied that she had slept at the Hampton House. That was an unusual answer: Most people reply with the name of a city, county or state. He asked where she was headed, and she said she was going to a small town to see a friend. What small town? he asked. Bel Air, she said. Verzi worked out of Bel Air; it was a town of about 8,000 people roughly three miles east of the cornfield.

Verzi asked for the name of the friend she was going to visit, and Amy replied that she would rather not get anyone else involved in what she termed "this situation." He asked what she meant by that. "This is a traffic stop," he reminded her. "This is not a 'situation' at this point." Amy shrunk into herself, avoided looking at his eyes, peered down at the floor—and changed the subject. She said she was buying a house in the area. Her story was falling apart. First she'd said she was sight-seeing; then she said she was there to buy a house. She had a friend in the area, but wouldn't identify him or her.

Verzi asked again if she had any drugs, weapons or large amounts of cash in the car. Amy paused, looked down at the floorboard again and said: "Well, I have some money. And it's my money."

How much money?

"A couple of thousand," she said. Verzi asked what she meant by "A couple of thousand." She said $5,000, and volunteered that it was from her business. Verzi wanted to know why she hadn't told him about the money the first time he asked, and she said it was because she'd learned through watching television that police seized money from people. Verzi explained that the money wouldn't be seized if she wasn't carrying drugs or other contraband in the car and if she had a valid reason for having it.

In response to another question about her business, she said she was in sales. Verzi asked what she sold, and she said she had a carpet and upholstery cleaning business in Las Vegas. Amy had committed another blunder. Carpet cleaning wasn't sales. It was a service. She was doing far too much dancing around, and her story was rapidly fragmenting.

Verzi wanted to pin down exactly what kind of business she was really involved in, and he asked if she had a business card. Amy said she did, and once more began shuffling through the maps and papers in the glove compartment. She couldn't find the card. "It's in the trunk," she said.

That was another bad mistake. At that point, the suspicious police officer didn't have a search warrant or, put in strictly legal terms, didn't have probable cause to arrest her or to order her to open the trunk. But if she voluntarily opened it, there were no restrictions in the law that prevented him from peering over her shoulder while she poked around inside. So that's exactly what he did.

Amy took the keys out of the ignition, got out of the car and walked to the back and opened the locked trunk. A half-dozen or so pieces of luggage were inside, and Amy went through one of the suitcases without any success in finding a business card. The second trunk she searched yielded a business card, which she shakily handed to him. It said "DeChant & Company." It was for a carpet and upholstery cleaning company in Las Vegas.

As soon as she opened the trunk, the officer made a couple of quick observations that started alarm bells ringing in his mind. The spare tire didn't have a rim on it, and the carpet that lines the trunk was pulled away from the walls where it hooks into the molding. The large screws that hold the carpeting were also pulled out. In addition to his hands-on experience undercover and later in drug interdiction, Verzi had undergone considerable specialized training with the FBI, and the Drug Enforcement Administration (DEA), as well as various agencies in other states, so the conditions inside the trunk evoked an immediate gut feeling that the Bonneville may have been used for shady dealings.

Verzi and fellow officers had previously arrested couriers who stowed drugs in spare tires or pulled up the carpeting in car trunks and secreted the contraband in specially fashioned hidden compartments. The carpeting almost never fits back into place perfectly after it has been pulled up, and loose edges and ends can provide a tell-tale clue that some monkey business is going on. Verzi concluded that enough factors were present to warrant a reasonable suspicion that the driver was a drug courier and justify calling in a narcotics-sniffing dog.

He'd missed an earlier opportunity to call in a dog, primarily because of the isolation of their location. They were deep in farm country and there wasn't even a house in sight. According to Maryland law, a drug-sniffing dog could be called to scan the exterior of a vehicle stopped for a traffic violation, but under normal circumstances must finish with its job by the time checks have been made on the driver's license and the citation written out. Police were not allowed to detain drivers any longer than it would take them during a normal vehicle stop. But there was an exception. If the officer has constructed enough factors to back up a claim of reasonable suspicion that would stand up under the scrutiny of defense attorneys and the court, he or she could hold the suspect long enough for the dog to arrive and do its work.

Verzi told Amy that he was going to call for a canine to sniff the vehicle and check for drugs. Amy said there weren't any drugs, but Verzi had made up his mind. He told her he was going ahead with his plan to call for the dog, and directed her to get back inside the car and sit down. While Amy slipped back into the front seat of the Bonneville and sat down, Verzi got busy on his police radio talking with the communications section of the Harford County Sheriff's Department, then with surrounding police agencies. None of them had a drug dog working in the area at that time. He finally located a dog living with a Harford sheriff's officer clear across the county, about forty-five minutes away. It was a good, experienced dog certified in drug detection. Verzi and the woman in the car faced a long wait.

It was difficult for Amy to sit still with no one to talk to for that long, and she got out of the car a couple of times to chat with the police officer. Verzi asked her to get back inside the Pontiac. The road was narrow and he didn't want to take any chances that she would be hit by a car. Almost over-cooperative, she reluctantly complied. By that time, two more patrol cars had pulled over behind Verzi's. His backup was on the scene at last, and one of the newly arrived officers was a woman.

While Amy resumed her silent vigil in the driver's seat, with her skirt modestly arranged back in place just above her knees where it belonged, the police sergeant kept his eye on her. He noticed that she was moving around in the seat and reaching over to the floor on the passenger side of the vehicle. Verzi walked quietly over to the passenger-side window, while Amy continued to reach toward on the floor, her eyes on the driver's-side mirror. Verzi was out of her view just behind the door post on the other side of the car when she picked up a blue plastic bag. Then she caught a peripheral vision glimpse of the police officer watching her, jerked in alarm, and in what was a mostly reflexive action tossed the bag back down.

Amy's nerves were still on edge, and she fidgeted, peered into the mirrors to see what the police officers were doing behind her, and began rummaging again in the glove compartment. One of Verzi's colleagues noticed her fussing around with an eyeglass case inside the glove box. Amy had said she didn't have a gun and none of the officers saw any trace of a firearm, but it wasn't unusual for drug couriers to be armed in order to protect their investments. Neither Verzi, nor his colleagues wanted to take any unnecessary chances, and they kept a close eye on the woman in the car, especially when she was moving around.

About forty-five-minutes after Verzi located an available drug-sniffing dog and almost exactly one hour after he stopped the speeding Bonneville, the canine and its handler pulled up in their vehicle. The isolated little stretch of Maryland Highway 23 was starting to take on the look of a busy used car lot with four police vehicles and the Pontiac parked at different angles along the side of the road, and a half-dozen people and a dog at the scene. The few motorists who drove by were quickly waved on by one or more of the officers almost before they could slow down and crane their necks at the curious assembly.

Even after all the demanding qualifications for calling in a drug-sniffing dog were met by Verzi, the animal and its handler continued to be restricted in their work by a quixotic set of rules. Lawmakers might be difficult to fathom if they weren't all politicians and so many of them weren't lawyers, but those factors, which exist in every state, probably explain why criminal codes are so complex, awkward and often seemingly tipped heavily in favor of suspected criminals. According to Old Line State criminal codes, the drug dog could sniff the outside of the car, but couldn't break the threshold of the vehicle unless the animal gave a positive alert during its inspection of the exterior.

The dog alerted in the area of the rear bumper and trunk, indicating the possibility of a controlled dangerous substance. That provided the necessary legal go-ahead for officers to search the car. At that point, if they wished, they could impound the car, tear out carpeting, padding, sidewalls, remove seats and generally dismantle it. They could also direct the dog to sniff any area of the vehicle's exterior and interior they wished, and the driver and all passengers could be personally searched.

The situation was out of Amy's control, and there was nothing she could do but follow orders and stand helplessly by as the troop of police officers piled up one suspicious discovery after another. There would be no games of hide-and-seek with police while camping at the homes of friends, and no telephone negotiations. The seemingly minor bobble that led to a speeding ticket had mushroomed into a nightmare, and her troubles were just beginning.

Verzi and his colleagues still didn't know if she was armed, and after the dog's alert outside the car and with a woman officer on the scene, they were at last able to see for themselves. The police sergeant asked Amy to get out of the car, and she assumed the classic stance with her hands on the roof and her legs spread-eagled while the female officer patted her down. Amy was wearing a fanny pack, and it had a suspicious hard lump inside about the size of a fist. The woman officer unzipped the fanny pack and removed a huge wad of money secured with a rubber band.

The currency was all in crisp $100 bills separated into lots, then covered with a rubber band. Each of the little packages was folded into other packages, so that they overlapped, then bound together with another rubber band. After removing the fanny pack, the officers counted $19,000. When Amy was asked why she had such a large sum of currency in a fanny pack, she replied that it was money from her business and she was afraid they were going to confiscate it. Verzi asked if there was any more money in the car.

"Well, I guess you're going to find it anyhow," she said. "I have about a hundred in the car."

"What do you mean by a hundred?" the officer asked.

"About a hundred thousand dollars," she replied. Amy said the money was all over the car, some of it in a bag with her food. Fast-food trash is another bellwether tip-off to an alert police officer that a driver has been eating in her car, and fits into the profile of a drug courier.

Still trembling and looking as forlorn and miserable as a wet housecat, Amy watched helplessly while the police officers searched the Pontiac and began collecting the money she had hidden. Money, almost all crisp, newly designed $100 bills recently issued by the U.S. Mint, was everywhere: smeared with ketchup and stuffed in fast-food sacks along with half-eaten food, under the floor mats and in a money belt.

The officers were finding so much money that they decided to move the Bonneville to a secure location on police property in Bel Air where they could do a more complete search. They called for a flatbed truck to haul the car away, and drove Amy to the sheriff's department headquarters to wait while the search was completed. At that point, although she was surrounded by police and they had taken possession of the vehicle, she still wasn't officially under arrest.

The search of the Bonneville was eventually resumed at the crime laboratory in Bel Air, but it wasn't underway very long before startling new discoveries led officers to call a temporary halt. Opening a wrinkled paper sack, they found a couple of items. One was a clipping from a Las Vegas newspaper about the investigation into Bruce Weinstein's disappearance. The other was a hurriedly scrawled note that appeared to have been written to a male friend by the woman driver of the vehicle. The message basically indicated that she was a suspect in a murder.

The note concluded with the words: "Amy on the run."

Verzi returned to his office where he telephoned the homicide division in Las Vegas and asked to speak with the lead investigator on the Weinstein case. Detective Bigham responded, and the two officers agreed that they should seek a search-and-seizure warrant from the local Maryland courts to continue the examination of the Pontiac for evidence. Bigham told Verzi that he would fly to Maryland and join in preparation of the application for the warrant.

Amy was officially placed under arrest and processed into the Harford County Detention Facility. She was charged by the Harford County State's Attorney's Office with processing drug proceeds. Amy was faced not only with an immediate loss of freedom, but, if the State's Attorney proved the case against her, the money found in her car and in the fanny pack could be confiscated as drug proceeds. The woman who had falsely sought to demonize a man by intimating that he was involved in shady big-time drug deals, was herself now locked up in a backwater Maryland county jail, suspected of violating narcotics laws.

That evening, Bigham and crime-scene analyst Michael Perkins caught a red-eye flight from McCarran International in Las Vegas to the Baltimore–Washington International Airport in Anne Arundel County, Maryland, where they rented a car and drove the twenty-five miles to Bel Air.

After the search-and-seizure warrant was obtained, Bigham and Perkins were joined by Verzi and local crime-scene analyst Diane Newton. Then they conducted a stem-to-stern inspection of the Pontiac Bonneville, the luggage and other items stored inside. Items collected and tagged by the search team included a shovel that Verzi had previously observed in the trunk, more currency, wigs, a passport in the name of Amy DeChant, a bagful of documents relating to Amy's legitimate business activities, and other, more intriguing paperwork.

A copy of a birth certificate for a woman named Robin R. Phillips raised law enforcement eyebrows. The birth certificate, which carried a pair of baby footprints but no photograph, indicated that she was born in Virginia on October 17, 1961—more than thirteen years after Amy was born, but Amy could probably have passed herself off as a thirty-five-year-old woman.

Applications for a Social Security card and a driver's license were also made out in the name of Robin R. Phillips, and were filled out with the same birth date that appeared on the birth certificate. The driver's license listed the height of the applicant as five-foot, three-inches, and her weight as 115 pounds. Amy's specs matched precisely. There was considerable reason to suspect that she may have been planning to create a new identity for herself.

Amy's penchant for scribbling notes had helped cast suspicion on her before, and it came back to haunt her again during the traffic stop and subsequent car search. At one point during the confrontation with Verzi, Amy had stuffed a handful of papers into her mouth and started chewing them up. Police pried her mouth open and retrieved the slobbery mess, but the notes were in bad shape. In the condition they were in they were unreadable, but that would be changed.

Several intriguing handwritten notes were found, including: "S.S. ID for next trip." Other notations listed the words *voters card*, *telephone bill*, *lease*, *library card*, *church*, *doctor's exam* and *drivers license*. The name and telephone number of Tom Dillard, a private detective in Las Vegas, also appeared in the notes, with the reminder, "Ask voice mail, tap and trace access." An outline, or script, of Amy's story about the four thugs who reputedly invaded the house in Las Vegas and murdered Bruce, was also found in the car.

Although a secret compartment was discovered under the dashboard, no drugs were turned up by the search team. Verzi later said during grand jury testimony in Las Vegas that he and other law officers believed Amy had already dropped off a load of drugs and was returning to New Jersey when she was stopped for speeding. The veteran narcotics cop also conceded that residue or odors from narcotics transported months earlier could have been responsible for the dog's drug alert. Odors seep into the fibers of upholstery and other areas of a vehicle and can be detected by drug-sniffing dogs long after illegal substances have been removed.

Bigham tried to talk to Amy after the search of the car was completed, but as he described it later, "She was already lawyered-up."

Although Amy refused to talk to Bigham, she agreed to meet with Wysocki when the private detective visited her at the jail. Because his activities were privately funded by Bruce's family, he was able to spend much more time in Maryland than Bigham and Perkins, who left for home after a near–non-stop three days of activity conducting searches and interviews. Wysocki was brought up-to-date on the car search and some other aspects of the Maryland investigation by local officers before sitting down to talk to the woman he had been tracking for so long.

The PI was surprised at Amy's appearance. The stress of the past few weeks was showing, compounded by her sudden detention behind bars, but the most dramatic change in her appearance was her hair. It was dyed dark brown and cut in a short shag extremely close to her head. The prisoner still had a bit of the appearance of a mischievous pixie, but it was the look of a very tired and frazzled pixie, incongruously dressed in a rumpled Harford County Detention Facility jumpsuit that was too big for her. She shrunk sullenly into the baggy jail uniform, far from her usual flirtatious self.

The private detective commented about her new hairdo, and she told him she simply became tired of the old look and decided to cut it short. When Wysocki asked her about the wig found in the car, she said she didn't like her new haircut. Then she indignantly reminded him that it wasn't against the law to have a wig or to wear one.

Wysocki had been put in his place by Amy before, and he rolled with the punches. It was part of his business. He pushed ahead with the interview, asking her about the documents carrying the name of Robin R. Phillips and other material that investigators suspected was part of a scheme to obtain false ID. Amy shrugged her shoulders. She didn't want to talk about it.

She also didn't want to talk about the money found in the car, which amounted to $101,000 when it was all collected and counted by Verzi and other sheriff's officers. About all she would say to Wysocki on the subject was that it was hers. She reminded him that she had a very successful business. When the private eye pressed her for more information about the money, she simply looked at him, shrugged and changed the subject.

Amy stubbornly denied that she had anything to do with transporting or selling illegal substances, and insisted she didn't know why authorities were accusing her of such terrible things.

Efforts by Wysocki to get her to tell him more about Bruce's murder were similarly fruitless. She stuck to the same scenario she'd told him before about four gangsters with New York accents bullying their way into the house and killing her boyfriend. That was her story and she wouldn't budge.

Wysocki began peering into bushes and around corners, working to develop a picture of Amy's activities in Maryland before her arrest. Following up on the discovery of rent receipts during the search of the Pontiac Bonneville, Wysocki learned that Amy had already rented a house under another name and was busy creating a new identity for herself. One time when she was sitting in a roadside restaurant she spotted a lawn care truck and asked the operator for a receipt for work done at the new residence. He'd never worked at the residence, but she was an attractive woman, had an enchanting line of patter, and he obliged. He wrote the receipt out listing the name, address, and date that she provided. The receipt was designed to show that she had lived in the house for a while, and represented one more building block in the task of creating a new identity for herself.

When Bigham and Perkins flew back to Las Vegas, the money confiscated from Amy's car stayed behind in Maryland. The currency became tied up in jurisdictional rivalries and emerged as a source of discord almost as soon as it was counted. The Las Vegas detectives wanted to take it back home with them as evidence in their homicide investigation, and lower-level officers in Bel Air weren't initially opposed to that. Other authorities in Harford County reportedly became involved, however, and claimed the money should stay there as evidence in their case against the Las Vegas woman. U.S. government drug enforcement officials were also interested in the money because of possible violation of federal laws. The entire situation was a mess, and not something that the out-of-town cop from Las Vegas had the authority or clout to work out by himself.

The homicide detective was already disappointed because the bills were counted and rebundled before he arrived in Maryland. Bigham had learned from Mrs. White about the distinctive fold Bruce had used to keep his on-hand currency in neat $1,000 lots, with $500 folded one way, and another $500 folded the other way, joined together and tied with rubber bands. Sheriff's officers in Bel Air, of course, didn't know about the importance of the fold, so they simply removed the rubber bands and counted the money, then rebundled it.

Bigham asked Perkins to take some photographs of the currency anyway. While Perkins was snapping pictures, a senior Harford County officer walked by and exploded in anger. He said the cash should already have been placed in a bank account where he claimed it would be better protected than in their safe—and it would be collecting interest.

Police didn't have the hard evidence they needed to back up suspicions that the money was tied to some kind of big-time drug deal, and most of it was eventually returned to Amy. According to a negotiated forfeiture worked out by federal authorities, Amy got about seventy-five percent of the money back, officials in Las Vegas later indicated. Money that she could firmly account for with receipts and other proof was returned to her. She needed it. One of the first people she talked to after her arrest in Bel Air was a lawyer known locally for representing defendants suspected of drug offenses, according to Bigham. And she would have other, even more extensive legal fees to pay in the future.

Although Bigham and Perkins didn't leave Maryland with the $101,000, they didn't return to Las Vegas empty-handed. They carried evidence gathered in the car search, and a little bag full of the torn and chewed-up notes that Amy was forced to spit out. The notes were turned over to crime laboratory technicians, who had them rehydrated, then redried and pieced together so they could be studied by a handwriting expert. The hard work paid off, and enough recognizable words were eventually restored to identify the material as notes about establishing ID.

Amy's arrest in Maryland made the news in Las Vegas, even though she still wasn't charged with any offenses involving Bruce's disappearance or suspected death. The *SUN* reported that Amy was jailed on drug charges in Maryland, and was a suspect in the murder of a missing professional gambler in Las Vegas.

Amy remained in the county jail for nearly two months before her bail was reduced from $2 million to $5,000. Her brother, Mickey Gerber, posted $5,000 cash bail, and Amy walked out of the detention center on September 13, a free woman once more.

On Sunday, less than one week before her release, Amy had telephoned her old friend Roy Seider, whom she had worked with at the former Vegas World casino and told him she was coming back. She said she wanted to clear her name because she was innocent.

CHAPTER TEN

OLD ALAMO ROAD DOE

"... and I mean, I didn't know why I was
going to the grand jury, but I have no other
problems in my life besides her."
—KEITH LEROY BOWER
FORMER BOYFRIEND OF AMY DECHANT

On August 11, almost five full weeks before Amy was released from the Harford County Jail, Las Vegas Metro Police logged in a phone call from a rabbit hunter who
reported that he and a friend had found a body near the
northern tip of Lake Mead, some sixty miles from the city.
A dentist and a relative of a Metro policeman were riding
in an all-terrain vehicle along a barren stretch of desert
when they were attracted to the remains by a nasty odor.

The homicide division rotation was seriously backed up
with live-case investigations of dead people, and by the
luck of the draw, the new case was assigned to Detective
Thowsen.

Tramping around in the desert between Las Vegas and
the heat-parched little settlement of Overton while medical
examiners and crime-scene analysts worked around a decaying body was an unpleasant way to spend a Sunday
afternoon. But it was Thowsen's turn in the rotation, and
he climbed into his car to begin the long drive to a sun-

baked bit of badland just off Old Alamo Road in northern Clark County.

Thowsen drove past Nellis Air Force Base, heading in the general direction of the Muddy Mountains and the sandstone cliffs in the Valley of Fire State Park, until he pulled his dusty car to a stop about a half-mile west of State Route 168 and climbed out. There wasn't much to see except brambles, gravel, a few tiny cactuses closely hugging the desert floor—and a small knot of men already gathered around a shallow grave at the bottom of a ravine about ten yards or so from the road. A dune buggy was parked a few feet away.

It wasn't much of a grave, and there wasn't much left of the body, except for the godawful smell. The experienced cop's work had brought him in close contact with long-dead bodies before, and the odor was as unforgettable as it was unmistakable. It wasn't the normal cloying putrid odor of decaying flesh that was so overpoweringly strong that it clung to clothing and skin long after the body was carted away to the morgue. The remains of the body half sticking out of the puddle of yellow and brown gravelly dirt was different. The odor it gave off was strangely sweet and metallic, and so harsh that it made the eyes burn. It was later thought that industrial cleaning fluid had been used to speed up decomposition, resulting in the burning smell and the stains.

The pitiful clump of dried-out bones were held together by scraps of leathery brown skin and silver duct tape tied around the wrists and ankles. A thick mass of long hair that was a curiously ugly shade of red was attached to the skull. Although Thowsen and his colleagues at the scene meticulously policed the area for several hundred yards in every direction, there was no trace of clothing, weapons, or any other immediately obvious detritus linked to the pitiful object in the grave. There were no cigarette butts, no chunks of rock with suspicious, rusty blood-like stains, no beer cans—nothing that appeared to be a potential clue. The victim seemed to have been killed elsewhere, then transported to the Old Alamo Road site and dumped naked inside the makeshift grave.

Whoever left the body there didn't even bother to scratch out a hole, but had obviously rolled or dropped it into the ravine, then dumped it in a small natural depression and piled a few large rocks and gravel on top. The gravesite was about as lonely and remote as it could be. Old Alamo Road was a beat-up two-lane highway leading miles north to Alamo, a gritty little desert settlement of about 250 people in neighboring Lincoln County.

Almost no one used the road anymore. The occasional motorists with an inclination to head up that way usually drove north on U.S. Road 93, which extends right through the town and continues all the way into Idaho. U.S. 93 was a modern, well-maintained highway, unlike Old Alamo Road, which had clearly seen better days. About every quarter-mile, huge chunks of the paving were washed away, and there was hardly any traffic—until the rabbit hunters stumbled across the body.

Thowsen talked with the hunters, and jotted down their names, the approximate time of the discovery, and other pertinent details. Amazingly, while the men were returning to the site after telephoning police they stumbled across another body dumped a short drive from Morman Peak. The second body and the peak were in adjoining Lincoln County about a mile north of the first set of remains, which were discovered in Clark County. It seemed there were more bodies hidden in the wasteland around Las Vegas than jackrabbits or desert cottontail. The second case was investigated by Lincoln County authorities, and it was eventually determined that the two murder victims were not linked to each other. Their only connections were discovery on the same day, by the same pair of rabbit hunters.

It's not unusual for bodies to be found among the sagebrush, rocks, prickly fishhook cactus, and gravel of the arid desert that surrounds Sin City. During one five-month period in the mid-1990s, twelve bodies were discovered, including three unidentified middle-aged Asian women who had been stabbed to death.

Crime Scene Analyst Daniel Holstein and colleagues from the Metro PD measured the grave off Old Alamo Road, used the sparse landmarks available in the isolated patch of desert to triangulate distances, shot photographs, and sifted through gravel. As the group of men worked around the remains in the fifteen-foot ravine, the western sky filled with soft pastels, then brilliant gold and orange streaks, and the scene around the gravesite was rapidly overtaken by shadows. Early evening chill replaced the blistering heat of the day.

The contrast between the solitary beauty of the desert and the horror of the grisly work underway went unnoticed and uncommented upon by the men gathered at the scene. Homicide detectives, crime-scene analysts and medical examiners are used to working around dead bodies, with their blood and bile and disagreeable odors. The odors can be the worst, or at least the most personally problematic, partly because they so persistently stick to clothing. Detectives and other people working closest to crime scenes are issued special khakis. The professionals who wear them call them "BDUs," Battle Dress Uniforms. BDUs are also worn when police are called to search for drowning victims or to recover floaters at nearby Lake Mead or in the Colorado River that flows into and out of the lake.

Three or four of the men working in the stifling dry heat

of the ravine were dressed in BDUs. Others who joined the growing knot of people watching the action from the rim of the ravine were dressed casually in T-shirts or open-necked sport shirts and lightweight slacks. Sergeant Hefner of Metro's Homicide Unit, and a couple of people from the morgue were among the observers.

The remains of the victim were in such bad shape that investigators couldn't immediately determine if they belonged to a male or female, or to a white, black, or Oriental. The dentist peered at the teeth and said they looked like they belonged to someone in their late teens, about eighteen years old. Based on the dentist's casual observation, Thowsen figured the victim may have been a street walker, or some other young woman who got herself tangled up in Las Vegas's roaring vice business as a nude model, exotic dancer or employee of one of the scores of Las Vegas escort services, but that was just a theory. Medical examiners, and perhaps other experts, would have to study the skull, pelvis, and other bones before the sex of the victim could be exactly determined.

After crime-scene analysts were finished with their duties, and the deputy county coroner completed his on-the-scene observations, the exhumation team began their morbid work. The exhumation was professional and deliberate. The technicians lifted the body gently and carefully, making sure not to leave even a tooth or a sliver of bone behind. An adult body is equipped with 210 bones to make the structure work. Bodies left long enough on their own so that they decompose often have many or several bones missing. They may be carried off by animals, washed away, scattered during rainstorms and other harsh weather conditions, or merely missed and left behind when the rest of the remains are exhumed.

The excavators didn't merely lift the desiccated bones

from the grave and drop them in a body bag, but removed the stones piled on top of the remains one by one, then carefully dug away the dirt and gravel. Every precaution was made not to disturb evidence that might be under or around the dismal clutter of chalk-brown bones in the makeshift grave.

The men worked quietly, and the stillness of the desert was unbroken except for an occasional intake of breath or grunt from their exertions. No one heard so much as a peep from an elf owl, or the startled rustle of a cactus mouse. The dry, dusty strip of desert was as still as death.

It was night when the remains were at last placed on a clean sheet inside a black body bag, and secured with a blue Clark County Coroner's Office seal stamped with an identifying number. Then they were loaded into a waiting hearse, and transported to the morgue in Las Vegas. The sheet was later closely inspected for any bits of evidence that may have fallen off the body. Crime-scene analysts dug down several inches beneath the body to make certain there was no clothing, bones, or other possible bits and pieces of evidence underneath. They didn't find so much as a cigarette butt.

Before leaving the ravine, Thowsen spent some time inspecting a stain at the bottom of the gravesite. It didn't look like the smudges typically left behind by body fluids found around decomposing corpses. It looked wet, dark, and a bit like the dirty puddle made when someone drives into the desert to drain the oil from a car. At Thowsen's request, samples of the soil and sparse vegetation were taken from the grave for later analysis.

After the remains were transported to Las Vegas and removed from the hearse at the morgue, they were processed into the system. The weight was recorded as about ninety-five pounds, then the bag was placed, still sealed, into a cooler to await autopsy. The seal was kept in place to protect the evidence, and for the vital purpose of maintaining the chain of custody. If the chain of custody was violated, at some later time when a suspected killer was put on trial for the murder of the person lifted from the desert grave, a skillful defense attorney could take advantage of the miscue and possibly prevent a conviction.

On Tuesday, two days after the rabbit hunters stumbled onto the grave, Detective Thowsen, along with Detective Bigham and Crime Scene Analyst Dan Peterson, witnessed the grimly meticulous autopsy proceeding. Deputy Medical Examiner Dr. Robert Jordan conducted the autopsy with assistance from Kelly C. Morris, a senior forensic pathology technician. Before the fastening was broken and inspection of the remains could begin, a photograph was taken showing the seal still in place on the body bag. After the bag was opened another picture was taken, showing the toe tag with the name of the victim: Old Alamo Road Doe. The body weight was recorded again as ninety-five pounds, and the length at five feet, eight inches.

Hardly any soft tissue remained on the skeletonized corpse, and all the internal organs were gone, so there was no blood, bile, urine, stomach contents, or any of the other bodily fluids normally tapped for sampling and testing to deal with. Members of the autopsy team did the best they could with the bones, a bit of muscle tissue, and some hair.

Dr. Jordan found a chip fracture on the left eighth rib, which had the appearance of an injury caused by a bullet. The remaining soft tissue in the area was decomposed in a manner that suggested to the experienced pathologist that a certain amount of blood had been there at one time. It was an ugly mix of brown, green, and red, which is a characteristic sign of hemorrhage. A short time later, he discovered a medium-caliber bullet in a tiny bit of tissue on the left side of the chest, the opposite side from the damaged rib. Dr. Jordon reported that in his opinion the victim had died from a gunshot wound to the chest. And police had the bullet, although it was immediately obvious that it was in bad shape for ballistics comparisons.

The mutilated slug was photographed, cleaned of remaining soft tissue, and placed in an evidence bag before eventually being turned over to George Good, Sr., firearms and toolmark examiner for Metro police. Despite the poor condition of the slug, after performing a microscopic analysis, Good concluded that it was a .380-caliber copper projectile with a full metal jacket and rounded nose. It had been fired from an automatic. The determination was made by identifying a rifling of six lands and grooves with a twist to the left that are particular to .380's manufactured by Davis, Colt and a small handful of other companies.

As part of the autopsy process, two sets of X-rays, one known as physical X-rays and the other as dental X-rays, were taken of the teeth. There was no distinct evidence indicating that a head injury had occurred or contributed to the death. The skull was detached from the body during the autopsy, to be kept for further study or forensics comparisons with missing persons. There wasn't much of the strangely colored hair left on the skull, but Dr. Jordan said that there was enough to identify it as Caucasian. It was fine, long, and straight. The hair of blacks tends to be thicker and curlier, and Orientals have less hair than either of the other two major races.

There was a chance that at some point in an investigation, the skull might be used to reconstruct an image of the victim from kits with plastic overlays of noses, ears, eyes, chins, hairlines and other facial characteristics; a lifelike drawing by a skilled forensics artist; a three-dimensional image sculpted in clay; or used with a new high-tech computer program that reconstructs facial features. Photographs of the re-created face could then be reprinted in newspapers, shown on television and distributed in flyers. That wasn't a last resort, but it was still in the future if Old Alamo Road Doe remained unidentified for too long.

It took a while for some of the experts to make a conclusive call on the sex and race of the victim. It has been said of coroners that they speak the language of the dead, but the speech can sometimes be as challenging and difficult to decipher as the long-forgotten archaic tongue of a lost civilization.

Initially, doctors couldn't even determine the sex by looking at the pelvic bones, which most people believe is a dead giveaway. In textbook cases, the pelvic bones of females are generally wider than those of males, in order to accommodate the birth process. The skeletal remains of the person lifted from the desert wash on August 11, however, didn't fit classic descriptions.

Clyde Snow, the legendary forensic anthropologist from Texas, once said, "Bones are often our last and best witnesses: they never lie, and they never forget." The rest of the story, left unsaid, was that, in order to get bones to tell their tale, skilled interrogators are needed, men and women like himself: highly trained, experienced investigators who love the thrill of the chase, and know which guidelines to follow.

Skeletal clues for determining race can sometimes be as difficult to decipher as those used in figuring out the sex of a badly decomposed corpse. Guidelines are not always surefire rules for success, but they can help. The small cheekbones and straight facial profile on the skull fit the basic structural traits of a Caucasian. The femurs of Caucasians also have more curvature than those of blacks, which are generally flatter or straighter. The two temporal bones directly behind the ear were also large enough to indicate that the skull belonged to a male. Other giveaway traits in the bones were also recognized, and conclusively confirmed the race and sex of Old Alamo Road Doe.

The mistaken on-the-scene speculation that the remains belonged to a teenager or young woman wasn't that unusual. It's easy to err about matters of age, sex or race when a dessicated body has baked in the desert under a thin blanket of gravel and sand for a few weeks or months, and even the best-trained experts can have trouble.

Although police knew how Old Alamo Road Doe had died, and a forensic anthropologist made the final call on the race and sex, the experts hadn't unraveled all the secrets linked to the body recovered from the desert grave. Homicide detectives still didn't know who he was.

Old Alamo Road Doe was Thowsen's case, but he and Bigham were working hard to solve the mystery of Bruce's disappearance and presumed murder, and they didn't know that the solutions to the two puzzles were linked. Even though the remains were shown to be those of a white male, that fit the description of many missing men and suspected murder victims. Old Alamo Road Doe was basically ninety pounds of bones, a few more pounds of leathery skin and tissue, and a long shock of strangely colored red hair.

Police now knew the victim wasn't some unfortunate prostitute or other young woman, but it still looked like they might be investigating the slaying of a teenager. "The remains looked tiny. It looked like a tiny little person [sic] weighed 100 pounds," Thowsen later recalled. "It was just so tiny and fragile-looking."

The two homicide detectives were doing everything they could think of to find Bruce's body, but they were temporarily stumped. Bruce's photo had been run in local newspapers, shown on local television, and circulated on flyers. They had samples of his blood taken from the soiled mattress in the master bedroom, and had compared the DNA with that of his parents. Blood samples were taken from Fred and Sylvia White and sent to Cellmark Diagnostics, a private genetic testing laboratory in Germantown, Maryland. The Cellmark tests isolated the distinctive pattern of Bruce's genes, and as part of the process, confirmed that the Whites were his parents. But there was no corpse to compare the DNA to, so the samples were kept on file.

Mrs. White also contacted Dr. E. Thomas Jones, Bruce's dentist in Tarzana, California, whom he had continued to consult after moving to Las Vegas, and obtained a copy of the missing man's dental charts and X-rays. Dr. Jones had been treating Bruce since 1975 and provided a set of X-rays taken of his mouth on December 15, 1980. Mrs. White gave the charts to Wysocki, who passed them on to police.

Matching dental records with the unknown dead is a key element of the science of forensic odontology, the use of dental evidence to assist law enforcement and the courts. Forensic odontology has also been used to nab rapists and vicious serial killers through comparisons of bite marks on the human body, or on food such as a chunk of cheese, an apple, or chewing gum.

The most common use of forensic odontology is tied to cases like that of Old Alamo Road Doe, involving human remains that have been burned beyond recognition, grossly mutilated, or dismembered in accidents—or are in advanced states of decomposition after burial in isolated graves. Skilled odontologists are able to make determinations about age based on the amount of wear on teeth, the presence or lack of molars, and other factors.

But dental records are probably the most useful of all the tools they employ. Most adults have fillings or missing teeth, and they can provide the most useful guideposts to identifying a badly damaged body through dental records. Fillings do not deteriorate, although the tissue around them fades over time, and they are uniquely distinctive. Comparisons can be made by studying their shape and size. Even people without fillings can be identified through comparison of their teeth with dental charts, although it is a sophisticated process that requires great patience and care. Like fingerprints, no two teeth are exactly alike. In the courtroom, dental identification is as legally acceptable as fingerprints.

In Las Vegas one day, the two homicide detectives were kicking around theories about the Weinstein investigation, Old Alamo Road Doe, and other unsolved cases when Bigham got a sudden idea. "Hey, Tom, let's check our Old Alamo Road Doe X-rays against Bruce," he suggested. A few minutes later, Bigham and Thowsen were peering in amazement at a set of X-rays on a screen in the Homicide Unit offices. X-ray analysis and forensic odontology weren't their areas of expertise, but the match-up was unmistakable: Old Alamo Road Doe and Bruce Weinstein had the same dental patterns. A forensic expert from the crime lab inspected the X-rays from the dental records and compared them with those taken from the skull, and agreed. It looked like the remains recovered from the desert were those of the missing gambler. The sleuths were on the verge of solving one of the knottiest puzzles impeding their investigation into the Weinstein case.

Bigham was excited. He was hot on the trail and smelled blood. The detective made a quick telephone call to a local dentist who volunteered his help to Metro police as a forensic odontologist, spilled out a bit of the story and confirmed that he was in his office and available. Then Bigham and his colleague from the crime lab picked up the skull at the coroner's office, placed it in a sack, and carried it to the dentist.

Dr. Daniel Orr was waiting when they arrived, and the three men hurried into a back office, where they took new X-rays, then made comparisons with the records supplied by Bruce's dentist. It was a perfect match. The search for Bruce Weinstein was over. "We've always maintained from the beginning that he was murdered," Sergeant Hefner said when he announced the breakthrough in the Weinstein investigation to local news reporters.

The woman whom just about everyone who knew anything about the case believed was responsible for Bruce's murder had walked out of the Harford County Detention Facility in Maryland only two days before the body was identified. Talk was already going around that she was back in Las Vegas, or on her way. She already had a local lawyer representing her, Daniel Albregts, a well-known criminal defense attorney who knew the value of keeping a zipped lip. With the experienced legal eagle in her corner, it was unlikely that Amy would be playing any more telephone tag with the police, or talking with the press.

The discovery of the corpse's identity was a major development in the investigation, and confirmed the gloomy postulations of Bruce's family. Sergeant Hefner told a reporter for a story that appeared in the *SUN* the day after Bruce was identified, that Amy was a suspect in the case, although she hadn't been charged. Roy Seider, Amy's old friend and former poker room supervisor at the Vegas World casino, was still loyal. He told the reporter he couldn't "believe that she can do this." Cheryl Keyser was quoted in the same story as saying of her long-missing husband: "I've come to the conclusion that if he hasn't been in touch with me by now, he has to be dead."

Along with the cadavers of other John and Jane Does,

Bruce's remains were refrigerated and kept at the morgue to be claimed by family members if identified. Unclaimed bodies are eventually buried, but the skeleton dug up off Old Alamo Road was unidentified for only about one month, so it was still at the morgue. At last the Whites and Bruce's siblings could bury their son and brother, and get on with the long process of healing.

Almost 100 mourners gathered at Bunker's Mortuary and at Memory Memorial Park on Lone Mountain road to eulogize Bruce and say their final goodbyes. "My brother was both my partner and my best friend. Sometimes we fought, and as he tried to teach me about business, I tried to teach him about life," Steven Weinstein told the gathering. "I'll miss the screamin' and the schemin'. But most of all I'll miss my brother, Bruce. I will never forget him." Bruce's baby sister, Robin Loehr, told mourners, "I feel Bruce left this world with no guilt. He did exactly as he wanted to do. When you think of Bruce, please rejoice, and laugh at all the crazy, insane things he did."

Sylvia White brought up other matters when she talked to a journalist following the services. She said she felt better with the funeral over at last, and the pursuit of justice was on her mind. Mrs. White added that Amy was back in Las Vegas, and said she hoped she didn't run into her.

Mrs. White was correct about her son's suspected killer being back in town, but she looked different from the Amy DeChant that most people who knew her remembered. Robert Moon was working behind the bar at the Hacienda on Tuesday, September 17, less than a week after Amy was freed from the Maryland jail, when she showed up to see him. Amy walked into the casino wearing a long black wig and extremely dark sunglasses. Moon had never seen her wear a wig before, but he was expecting her, because a cocktail waitress had told him that Amy had appeared at the bar looking for him the previous day. The husky bartender wasn't enthusiastic about the meeting. Detectives had already called him in for questioning, and he didn't like the way Amy used and lied to him.

When she asked him to leave the bar for a few minutes to talk, he called the barback to take over. Amy said she was sorry for getting him involved in her troubles, and Moon responded that she could have telephoned to apologize. Amy claimed she was afraid to call, because she believed her phones and those of her friends were tapped. While they were talking, Amy's friend David joined them and listened in.

Amy finally got around to the serious business on her mind, and asked Moon about his interview with police. She especially wanted to know if they'd asked him about the safety deposit box at the Stardust. Moon confirmed that they had asked him about the box, and said he'd told them about driving her to the Stardust to open it. He'd also told them that she'd thought they were being followed when they drove there.

In what may have been a statement directed more to David than to Moon, Amy responded: "Well, we *were* followed." Amy insisted that she'd had nothing to do with Bruce's death, and was more afraid of his family than she was of police. Moon didn't hear from Amy again after the strained conversation at the bar, although David telephoned him a few times.

A big disappointment was waiting for Amy when she went to the Stardust to open the safety deposit box. Bigham had obtained a search warrant and beaten her to the punch. Investigators had already emptied the box of $35,000 in $5,000 race-sports chips—four from the Stardust and three from Caesar's Palace—and a collection of rings, watches, earrings, pearls and other womens' jewelry. (A judge eventually signed a court order permitting release of the casino chips to the Whites.) Discovery of the jewelry caught Amy up in another lie. She had claimed to have pawned it all. Bigham and his partners used bank records and information from witnesses to track down locations of safety deposit boxes she'd kept. They learned that she and her brother had signed in to open some of the lock boxes while Mickey was in town.

Amy had no legitimate reason to fear physical violence from members of Bruce's family, but they weren't through with her, or finished with their efforts to see that his killer, or killers, were brought to justice. One of the first orders of business, after burying their son and brother, was linked to the offers of reward money. Shortly after Bruce was identified, Bigham stood by while family members split the $25,000 reward offered for the recovery of his body between the two rabbit hunters who discovered the remains in the desert ravine.

There were other rewards still to be collected, including $10,000 that was still available to anyone who provided information leading authorities to Bobby Jones. Deputy Clark County District Attorney C. Dan Bowman had obtained a material witness arrest warrant for the frightened carpet cleaner, who had already been in hiding for more than two months since Fat Richie Reyes drove him across the desert to Kingman. Bobby's name had been on the NCIC computer since August.

Talk circulated in some circles that Bobby had been in New Mexico, Southern California, the Phoenix area, and in Las Vegas since he went on the lam. Richie Reyes saw him when he went to the Jones house for Thanksgiving dinner and found Bobby, home for the holiday. It was a relief to see him, Reyes later told authorities, because Bobby had been out of touch with his family in Las Vegas for so long that Reyes was afraid something had happened to him.

No one who knew where Bobby was hiding was talking to police, but investigators were steadily increasing the pressure. At exactly 3 o'clock on the afternoon of December 11, 1996, officers executed a search warrant for Bobby's house. Four members of the homicide division, including Bigham and Detective David Messinar, served the warrant. Messinar had become Bigham's new partner in the investigation after Thowsen was taken off the case to handle other pressing assignments.

The little yellow two-bedroom house with the covered carport at 136 North 19th Street was in an older section of Las Vegas, and was poorly kept up. Two of the address numbers on the outside of the single-family dwelling were missing, and only the "3" was still in place. At times, Bobby's son kept as many as three rattletrap cars sitting around in the yard, and other litter was scattered on the hard, sun-baked earth and dry, dead grass. The only people in the house when officers knocked on the door with the warrant were Bobby's stepdaughter, Suzanne Kathleen Antone, and her one-year-old son, Matthew, the youngest of her four children. The interior of the little house was a mess, with dirty clothes lying around on the floor, and dog and cat feces plainly visible. The chunky, green-eyed twenty-eight-year-old blonde said she hadn't seen or heard from her stepfather since he left town. She telephoned her mother at work to advise her that the police were there. Bigham also talked with Cheryl Keyser and told her why they were at the house, explaining that they were looking for anything that might help them locate her husband, Bobby. He also mentioned that they were looking for a murder weapon. Cheryl worked at Super Pawn, and Bigham was aware that most pawn shops did a big business in handguns.

In the affidavit the detective prepared as part of the application for search warrant, he specifically mentioned that he was looking for a .380-caliber handgun, bloodstained clothing, telephone records or other information indicating the possible whereabouts of Bobby Jones, cleaning supplies that were sufficiently caustic to accelerate the decomposition of a human body, and other items of personal property such as mail, photographs, leases, and utility bills helpful in identifying the occupants of the home.

Searchers didn't find a .380 at the house, but they discovered a .22-caliber pistol and a 9mm model 915 Smith and Wesson. They confiscated the Smith & Wesson because ballistically a 9mm is very close to a .380, and the officers wanted to be sure they weren't wrong about the caliber. The .22 was left behind, because investigators were looking for a higher-caliber weapon. They also seized a red address book with the names, addresses, and telephone numbers of family members and friends, a Christmas card that Cheryl Keyser had signed and directed "to Bob," a handwritten note stuck inside the card, various documents establishing residency, and a hand-drawn map with the address of relatives named as "Bob and Shirley" in Phoenix. Phoenix was one of the locations Bobby was thought to have visited during his high-stepping travels. Bigham left a copy of the inventory of the items seized during the search with Suzanne Anton.

Early in January, just a month after the search warrant was executed, a ten-year-old boy playing in the desert near the base of Sunrise Mountain in the eastern part of the valley discovered a pistol under a bush. Russell Seastrand didn't touch the dirt-and-rust-encrusted firearm, but took a good look at it before hurrying home and telling his parents what he had found. The boy had paid attention when a police officer with the DARE program visited his school and told the children that if they happened to see a gun somewhere, they shouldn't touch it, but instead tell their parents. DARE is an acronym for Drug Abuse Resistance Education, which is a nationwide program initiated in Los Angeles in 1983 that brings police officers into schools to help children learn to resist societal pressures to use drugs, alcohol and tobacco. Sometimes the DARE officers talk about other dangers, like guns.

Russell's father returned to the desert with his son, and confirmed the discovery of the approximately four-inch-long stainless-steel weapon with black trim. It was lying on the ground, as if someone had tossed it out the window of a passing car. There had been no attempt to bury it. The father returned to their house with his son and telephoned police. Patrol Officer William Chavera drove to the site to pick up the weapon. The patrolman secured it in an evidence bag, with a pair of red seals.

The little semi-automatic was a Davis Industries Model P.380, and fit the description of the type of handgun homicide detectives were seeking as the suspected murder weapon in the Weinstein case. Las Vegas Metro's firearms expert George Good was assigned the task of making the tests necessary to link the semi-automatic to the deformed bullet taken from Bruce's remains—or to rule it out. The firearm was heavily corroded, and there was no clip inside when it was found, but it was operable. Good used one of his own clips to test-fire it, manually ejecting the cartridge case after each shot. When he compared the test-fired bullets with the mutilated slug taken from Bruce's body, similar rifling characteristics showed up. It seemed to be a match.

Firearms specialists and other forensic experts are extremely careful about making judgments that they may not be able to back up with one-hundred-percent authority in court, where they can be submitted to scathing cross-examinations by defense attorneys. Words and phrases like "probable," and "could have been," or "very likely" can be lifesavers when the legal chips are down. Good eventually testified in a grand jury proceeding that "It's my opinion that this bullet may have been fired from this gun."

"Could have been?" he was asked. "Could have been," he agreed. Then he added, "It could have been fired from other firearms," and mentioned Davis, Colt, and other manufacturers that produce handguns with the same rifling characteristics.

Neither Amy nor Bobby knew anything about the development with the Davis P.380, but police were beginning to compile a strong circumstantial case against them, and were rapidly ratcheting up the pressure. In April, nine months after Bruce's murder, television's crime-fighting show, *America's Most Wanted* scheduled a segment on the search for Bobby Jones, and Bigham obtained court approval to place a wiretap on telephones in the house on 19th Street. The District Court order included approval of a trap-and-trace device to register the numbers of telephones used to dial in and out of the Jones residence.

Bigham was especially eager to monitor conversations following the *AMW* broadcast on April 12, when he expected the line to be busy with talk about the show. Homicide detectives monitored the wiretap until April 16, and didn't learn until later that the telephone company hadn't been able to get the trap-and-trace in place until the day the operation was shut down. The wiretap was a disappointment, but Metro homicide had plenty of other avenues to explore. Some of the most intriguing new leads were produced as a direct result of the television program.

Bigham had continued to develop new witnesses and interview people who had had contact with the fugitive carpet cleaner. A young woman, Lee Sue Steininger, and her father, Donald Steininger, were among the people who drove to the homicide division headquarters to talk with the determined detective.

Lee Sue, the former live-in girlfriend of Robert Raymond Jones—"Bobby Junior"—telephoned Bigham early one morning. The twenty-nine-year-old woman said that she had watched the program on April 12, and thought she should talk to police about her knowledge of her ex-boyfriend's father. Early that afternoon, she sat down with Bigham to tell her story. In her audio-taped statement, she said she had dated Bobby Junior for about three years before finally leaving him about a month earlier, and was living with him near Albuquerque in New Mexico the previous July when he told her that his father was in some kind of trouble over the disappearance of a man in Las Vegas. Sometime later she learned that the missing man had been murdered.

In her statement to Bigham, and during later grand jury testimony, the former waitress and casino card dealer said that the older man had lived nearby in New Mexico for a while and that his son had helped him hide out. Once, Lee Sue said, she had gone to California to visit her child, leaving her boyfriend by himself, and when she returned she noticed a chair in the living room that hadn't been there before. When she asked about it, Bobby Junior admitted that his father had been at the house.

Lee Sue said she subsequently saw a large amount of currency, about $10,000 in $100 bills, with a rubber band wrapped around it, but her boyfriend told her that he hadn't seen the money, and she hadn't seen the money. The implication was clear: she was expected to keep her mouth shut about the money, and forget she had seen it. Later, he claimed that the big wad of cash was money he'd saved from tips at work, she said. The stress of becoming involved with a wanted fugitive caused serious problems in the young couple's relationship, and Bobby Junior had beaten and threatened her. After they moved back to Las Vegas to live with her father, Lee Sue told the homicide detective, Bobby Senior had lived with them for a time.

When Bigham learned that Jones had stayed at the Steininger house in the 1000 block of Norman Avenue, he called Sue Ann's father to the Homicide Unit offices for a talk. Donald Steininger was cooperative and told the detective that he had first met Bobby Senior when he came to the house to visit with his son. The two older men became good friends, even though Steininger was aware that his new houseguest had had some criminal problems with the law. He promised Bigham that the next time he saw Bobby Senior he would try and talk him into surrendering to the authorities.

One of the new leads developed as a result of the broadcast on *America's Most Wanted* led homicide detectives back to Amy's old stomping grounds in New Jersey. Her former boyfriend, John Gerard, watched the program, then dialed the local New Jersey television station and said that he knew something about one of the people involved in the case. Station employees gave him the telephone number for the Las Vegas Metro Homicide Unit, and a short time later Gerard was talking with a detective.

Two detectives were sent to talk with Gerard, including David Messinar, but the lead investigator on the case didn't make the New Jersey trip. By chance, Messinar and Detective James Vaccaro were attending a week-long police homicide school at the New Jersey State Police Headquarters in Trenton in June, so they were instructed to rent a car and drive to Gerard's home in the Manor Crest Apartments in New Brunswick for the early-evening meeting. A

New Jersey state police detective sat in on the tape-recorded interview.

Gerard was still living in the same apartment and doing the same job at the Regency Manor, and he recounted the story of his business dealings and brief fling with Amy before she broke up with George Sackel and ran off to Detroit with the foreman. Then he got down to the serious business that had led him to contact homicide detectives about the toxic siren who'd cut a romantic swath through the local male population a decade earlier.

Amy had found herself another older man of means in Ohio when she contacted Gerard through his pager sometime in 1992, and said that she was having a problem with her beau's grown daughter. According to Gerard, Amy was "more or less running the business," but the daughter, who was about 21 or 22 years old, wasn't happy with the arrangement. Gerard said that Amy had wanted him to kill the old man for her.

"And, uh, she called me up one night and she wanted to know if I would fly in. She'd have a ticket for me, and she'd give me $20,000 to do him, to shoot him," Gerard said. The fretful witness indicated that he may have unwittingly set himself up for the offer, because he was a Vietnam veteran, and when he and Amy were hanging around together, he'd told her a few war stories. He speculated to the officers that she may have assumed he wasn't averse to doing a little killing, but if that's what she thought, she was dead wrong.

"I told her flat 'no,' and I haven't heard from her since," Gerard declared.

Responding to a question about why Amy wanted the old man killed, Gerard said it was because the daughter was interfering with the business and was going to be taking over. Amy indicated that her older boyfriend was wealthy.

During earlier conversations after Amy left New Brunswick, she'd told him about other men she'd hooked up with, the property manager said. They were always wealthy, and, Gerard told the detectives, it seemed that the money was the attraction for her.

"Did she ever tell you whether any of 'em turned up dead?" Gerard was asked. "No, she didn't," he replied. The property manager added in response to a follow-up question that he had never been to Las Vegas.

The detectives still hadn't firmly nailed down the motive for Amy's alleged scheme to have her older sweetheart murdered instead of the daughter, whom she had pinpointed as the person she was anticipating trouble with. How could Amy expect to wind up with the business if the old man was gone? they asked.

"It seems logical to me also, but, uh, knowing her, she— from George, she probably had the business in her name for the purpose or whatever," Gerard stammered. "She probably wangled everything."

CHAPTER ELEVEN

CLOSING IN

"She was smart. She was good-business–minded,
real money-hungry. She knew how to handle a dollar,
but pretty much, that was her whole life, was money."
—MICHAEL ANTHONY LUCARELLI
TO CLARK COUNTY GRAND JURY

Neither Bobby nor Amy seemed to be able to stay away
from Las Vegas for very long, even though they were seriously spooked by the television broadcast about the case.

For a while after returning to Sin City from Bel Air, and
weeks before the unsettling television show was aired, Amy
was shacked up with her faithful former boyfriend, Keith
Bower. The poker room shift supervisor still had a soft spot
in his heart for the quixotic woman who had left him because he couldn't afford her, and when she showed up looking for a place to stay, he told her she was welcome. They
resumed their old romance.

Police were still holding onto her Camaro Z-28 and the
work van, so she hitched rides with Bower, or used taxis
while she made the rounds of casinos—or lined up jobs for
her new business undertaking: Amy had established a
parking-lot-striping business. She bought a machine and
paint, and laid down the white or yellow stripes that set off
one space from another in parking lots.

She was hiding out in plain sight, spending hours on the telephone each morning drumming up business, going out to eat with her boyfriend, playing a little poker at the casinos and—after Bruce's body was identified—placing a call to Mike Wysocki. She started the conversation the same way she had most of their earlier talks, by bemoaning the fact that so many people suspected her of such terrible things, and insisting she was a victim. Then she abruptly changed direction and told the private eye, "That's not his body." The remark seemed to have come completely out of the blue, but that's how conversations with Amy were.

Wysocki responded that he understood Bruce was identified through dental charts. "I don't care," she insisted. "That's not his body, but I'm not going to say anything more."

One day, seemingly all of a sudden, she told Bower that she was moving out. Amy said that one of the cab drivers who had picked her up previously worked for Bruce or his family. She was afraid the cabbie would snitch on her, and that she would be set up for murder, she claimed.

Bower didn't know where she went, but a few weeks later she moved back in with him. Police had released the Camaro as evidence and returned it to her, but she couldn't afford living on her own, and complained that the expenses were eating her up. The reunion lasted a few weeks before she left again, but she didn't break off all contact. The complex, unpredictable woman left a telephone number for Bower to use for messages, and sometimes telephoned him. One night she called and announced that she was eating Mexican food—in Mexico. Another time she chatted about doing something or other on the East Coast, and also said that she had been playing poker down South.

Claudia McClure, the cleaning woman who had walked into the ambush by Wysocki and Bigham at the Stardust parking lot while trying to pick up the business files, had similar bewildering experiences. She loaned her car to Amy for a while, and was directed to a little motel to pick it up. When she arrived, Amy told her that she was leaving. Claudia asked where she was going, and Amy replied that she didn't want her to know. Dealing with Amy could be a bit like getting involved with the CIA: all secrets, covert actions, and rapidly changing addresses.

The two women made arrangements for Claudia to pick up Amy's mail and hold it for her. After a while, Amy agreed to have the mail sent directly to Claudia's house in order to save her friend the trouble of making repeated trips to the mail drop. Claudia quickly collected a boxful of envelopes, and forwarded some of the mail to an address in New Jersey. Amy instructed her to throw the address away, but Claudia eventually recalled that it may have been in Toms River. She said she thought it was probably the address of a go-between or third party.

Amy also left her friend a voice-mail number to get messages to her.

It was all very mysterious, and Claudia later said that she once talked with a detective who'd told her authorities were thinking of putting Amy in a witness protection program. Before Old Alamo Road Doe was identified, Claudia urged her friend to go to the police for help, but Amy said that police wouldn't protect her. Amy finally confided to her friend that a Mob hit had been carried out, and Bruce was dead.

Amy was apparently slipping in and out of town—unless she was feeding her friends a line of malarkey and never left Las Vegas—because she was seen by various acquaintances playing in Saturday-night low-limit poker tournaments at the Orleans, and hanging around other casinos. As it had been for Bruce, Las Vegas was Amy's kind of town.

Bobby Jones was doing some slipping and sliding around on his own, high-stepping between Las Vegas and parts unknown and getting away with it for ten months. On June 7, his gamble at last turned sour and the odds caught up with him.

Suzanne Anton's former boyfriend Alan Bady was the father of the youngest of her four children, and had agreed to babysit for her for a couple of hours the previous night so that she and her mother could go out and play bingo. The mother and daughter didn't return home until 5 a.m., and Bady didn't want to be on the street at that time of the morning, so he decided to stay where he was for a while— on the couch. He had lived with Suzanne three different times, so he knew the family and the house, and was comfortable there. It was like home.

Bobby Jones walked into the house about a half-hour after his wife and stepdaughter returned. Bady knew about the reward offer and realized that Bobby was worth a big chunk of money, so he waited a while, then slipped outside and made a telephone call tipping off the police. "He's there, right now," Bady said. Bady didn't go back to the house. Police did.

About 3 o'clock on a typically sizzling-hot afternoon, four or five black-and-whites and unmarked cars pulled up in the driveway in front of the shabby little house on North 19th Street. About a dozen police officers, some in uniform and some in plain clothes, piled out of the cars and took up positions around the yard. One of the officers knocked on the door, and when Cheryl Keyser answered, they told her they were there for her husband. She said that Bobby wasn't at the house, and she didn't know where he was.

While Bobby's wife stood outside in the blazing mid-afternoon heat with the police officers and a rapidly grow-ing crowd of curious neighbors, one of Bigham's colleagues telephoned him at home and told him what was going on. Bigham had a rare day off and was relaxing with his shoes off and his feet up on a footstool watching tele-vision. It took him about one minute to squeeze back into his shoes, climb in his car, and head for Bobby's house. It was normally a twenty-five- to thirty-minute drive, but Bigham made it in twenty.

When he arrived, everyone in the cast was still standing in the stifling-hot yard, except for Bady and the missing star of the drama, Bobby Jones. Bigham started talking to Cheryl about her husband, making sure his voice was loud enough so that anyone inside the house could hear. "Hey, look, if he didn't do anything, then he needs to come and tell us. If all he did was clean up, then he needs to tell us. If all that happened was he buried a body, if that's all he did, we can work things out."

He cautioned Cheryl that he knew Bobby had had guns in his possession before, because guns were in the house when the search warrant was served. "He needs to come out, because if something happens, he could be shot. It's a dangerous situation," the detective reminded her in his deepest, most forceful baritone. "We know he's involved in a homicide, and I know there's guns inside that house. Let's not escalate this thing." Bigham talked fast, and loudly enough that neighbors across the street could make out most of what he was saying. He kept it up until a tired-looking man with a heavy stubble of salt-and-pepper whis-kers opened the door. "Okay, okay, it's too hot to be standing around out here," the old man grumbled. The tense standoff was over, and no one had been hurt.

Bobby Jones looked exactly like what he was: a fifty-eight-year-old grandpa. He was balding, slightly dishevelled, and wearing a pair of casual slacks and an open-neck shirt. Police officers quickly grabbed his hands and pulled them behind his back, then snapped a pair of cuffs around his wrists.

Bigham took charge of the prisoner, and helped him into the back seat of his unmarked car. The burly homicide investigator started to say something about being ready to listen if Bobby wanted to talk, but barely got out a half-dozen words before the prisoner shrugged his shoulders. The message was clear enough, and Bigham read him the obligatory Miranda warning. A classic version of the rights, which in some jurisdictions is printed on cards in English and Spanish, advises:

"You have the right to remain silent. Anything you say can and will be held against you in a court of law. You have the right to talk to a lawyer and have him present while you are being questioned. If you cannot afford to hire a lawyer, one will be provided for you. Do you understand these rights?"

Almost every cop and many fans of police and crime shows on television knows the warning by heart, or they can come close to reciting it. It is read to suspected felons as a result of what is perhaps the most famous, some say infamous, U.S. Supreme court decision in the history of American criminal law. Ironically some years after the razor thin 5-4 decision in 1966 in Miranda-vs-Arizona, the controversial ruling may have protected a man suspected of killing the confessed kidnap rapist the landmark case is named after. Ernesto Miranda was retried and convicted after his confession to police was thrown out by the court, then released on parole in 1972. A short time later he was knifed to death in a bar fight in Phoenix. His attacker was questioned and released, and the crime is officially unsolved.

After running through the warning, Bigham repeated his offer to talk. "Hey, you hurt me outside the house there," the detective told him. "I can help you, but you gotta help yourself." Police and prosecutors had compiled a large amount of circumstantial evidence, but they didn't want to take any chances that the person they suspected of engineering Bruce's brutal murder might somehow beat the rap. They wanted a good witness. Bobby wasn't interested. "I want an attorney," he said. That was the end of the conversation, and Bigham drove his prisoner downtown to the Clark County Detention Center on Bridger Avenue at Casino Center Drive. Bobby was booked on the material witness warrant and assigned to a cell.

It wasn't exactly like old home week for the sullenly uncommunicative prisoner, but he had been behind bars in the twelve-story Las Vegas lockup before, when he got into a jam over child support. That time, Bobby Junior had ponied up the bail money, and Cheryl drove downtown with the cash to get her man out.

Police telephoned Sylvia White to relay the news of Bobby Jones's arrest. The grieving silver-haired mother said she was going to the cemetery to tell her son.

Bady met with representatives of the local Secret Witness program to collect his reward for dropping a dime on the man whose home he had lived in off and on during his sporadic relationship with Bobby's stepdaughter. Bigham watched while Bady opened an envelope containing the $10,000 reward that Bruce's family had posted for anyone who helped police track Bobby down. Bady's hands were shaking when he turned and looked at Bigham: "You remember I told you how much money Bobby had?" he asked. Grinning while he folded the bills over, he said, "That's as big as the amount of money he had."

Bobby was already free on $10,000 bail less than one

week later on June 12, when he was scheduled to testify before a Clark County grand jury in a matter titled "Investigation into the death of Bruce Weinstein."

When he reluctantly walked up to Prosecutors Chris J. Owens and Abbi Silver, waiting outside the closed grand jury room door on the fourth floor of the Clark County Courthouse, he wasn't happy about it. His mid-afternoon appearance was somewhat of a surprise because, although he had been subpoenaed, the prosecutors didn't know where he was or how to locate him. Bobby was with Cheryl Keyser, who appeared in some police reports as "aka Cheryl Jones," when he introduced himself about fifteen minutes before the proceeding was scheduled to begin.

Owens identified himself to Bobby and told him that he was subpoened to testify about his knowledge of the death of Bruce Weinstein. Bobby asked if he needed a lawyer. The deputy DA replied that he could talk to a lawyer if he wished, but it was up to him. The former carpet cleaner asked if the state would pay for the lawyer, and Owens told him that he would have to take care of the costs himself. Bobby then asked what his rights were, and Owens told him they were similar to the rights repeated so often on television, and specifically pointed out that he had the right to remain silent and that anything he said could be used against him in a court of law. The deputy DA told Bobby a second time that he had a right to refuse to testify, but that if he knew anything about Bruce's death he could choose to share the information with the grand jury. Bobby agreed to testify, and he didn't hire an attorney to consult with before going before the panel.

When he was questioned in Room 444 about his recent whereabouts, he said he had been driving a camper that belonged to his son. He'd returned to Las Vegas that morning because he wanted to see his wife. Bobby interrupted

Silver when she began to phrase a question about his earlier return to Las Vegas, which had led to his arrest after learning about the search warrant. He said that he hadn't known about the search warrant or the material witness warrant until he was picked up. The prosecutor started over. "I'm sorry. After the time you learned about . . . your home being searched, you didn't call the police at that time either?"

"No, ma'am, I did not," he replied.

A brief exchange then followed about whether he had been advised before testifying about his right to remain silent. Silver pointed out that he had talked about it with her colleague Chris Owens, but the witness claimed that he didn't remember being told he could choose not to testify. They also briefly discussed one of the handguns found by police during the search of his house, and he said he'd acquired the pistol as collateral for a personal loan. Bobby told the jurors that he didn't know anything about Bruce's murder, and the only thing he'd done was clean up a couple of juice stains from the carpeting in the house.

A week after Bobby testified, his wife Cheryl was called before the panel. Shortly after her appearance in Room 444, she and her husband vanished from their old haunts in Las Vegas.

When Paul Bigham and several of his colleagues served a second search warrant at the little house on North 19th Street, Suzanne Antone once again stood by while police officers spread out through the cluttered interior. She told the search team that her mother and stepfather were away, and she didn't know where they were or how to get in touch with them. The police officers were looking for the .22-caliber pistol they had seen during the previous search, other firearms, ammunition, cleaning equipment, and ownership manuals and documents to establish the financial condition of Bobby and his wife for the years 1995 to the present. In the affidavit for search warrant, Bigham said he had reviewed Bobby's criminal record. "Robert Jones is a convicted felon, and it is illegal for him to possess a firearm," the detective declared. Investigators confiscated the .22-caliber Stirling automatic and various documents. Bigham also obtained court approval to place a new trap-and-trace on the telephone at the same time the second search warrant was served.

When the grand jury was convened on August 14, 1997, to begin receiving additional testimony in the case styled *State of Nevada* vs. *Amy Rica DeChant and Robert Wayne Jones*, Chief Deputy District Attorney David J. J. Roger was at the helm. Roger was a member of the DA's elite Major Violations Unit, and one of Clark County's leading homicide prosecutors. He had compiled a sparkling record of convictions in some of the city's most high-profile cases.

In many ways, it might seem that Roger was born for the role of prosecutor—not the short-tempered, shouting, red-faced caricature of a DA so often seen fumbling away the big cases on television and on film, but the real-life version, a hard-driving, deeply committed servant of the people. Roger dresses conservatively, keeps his dark hair neatly trimmed, and looks like an accountant. In fact when he initially registered at the University of Nevada–Las Vegas, he was planning on a career as a CPA. After earning an accounting degree, however, he decided that number-crunching was too boring, so he enrolled at the California Western School of Law in San Diego, and graduated in 1986. He spent one summer doing tax law work but decided that that was also too dry, and concluded that he would be happier with litigation. While working as a law clerk in the Eighth District Court, he had an opportunity to watch some of Clark County's top prosecutors in action and realized that they were doing exactly what he wanted to do. He applied for a position, and has been on the staff ever since.

Like all the newcomers at that time, he was assigned to a circuit on a three-week rotation, handling preliminary hearings in the city of North Las Vegas for one week, then moving to Henderson to do the same thing, and during the third week working misdemeanors and drinking-and-driving cases.

Young DAs worked at that job until a prosecutor senior to them either went into private practice, retired, or died. Roger's timing was good, and in the early 1990s he was assigned as one of the three prosecutors with the Major Violations Unit, handling all the murder and other high-profile cases in Clark County.

At the time he was assigned the Weinstein homicide in 1996, he had represented the state on sixty-four trials and lost only four overall. "It's always a fascinating job prosecuting people who have done the unspeakable crimes," he says. "And I love my job."

The prosecutor's training as an accountant is reflected in his approach to a murder trial; he is most comfortable dealing with factual matters and absolutes. It's like working with numbers.

Police officers, and other law enforcement professionals who rub shoulders with him, like the way he works. "He's a pleasure to do pre-trial with," Bigham observed of the Chief Deputy DA. "When he starts a new case he reaches in one drawer and pulls out a brand-new pen, then he goes in another drawer and pulls out a fresh notepad. Everything with him is organized, and carefully controlled. There's no clutter. He doesn't leave loose ends."

The grand jury testimony in Room 444 of the courthouse extended into September, while Roger and his colleagues patiently built their case around the rapidly growing mound of evidence being accumulated by police and prosecutors.

By that time, neither Bobby nor Amy could be located by authorities. Amy wasn't even telephoning Wysocki any more. Consequently, the court waived the statutory notice requirements for Bobby, and Amy's lawyer, Daniel Albregts, agreed to accept his client's notice on her behalf. As part of the agreement with Albregts, the District Attorney's Office agreed to give her forty-eight hours to turn herself in if the grand jury returned an indictment against her.

One of Roger's most important jobs during the proceeding was establishing that the rusty Davis .380 that police had recovered from the desert was the likely murder weapon, then linking it to Bobby Jones, and through him to Amy.

Twenty-five-year-old Matthew Hunt testified that he had sold or given the firearm to Bobby Junior when the two young men worked together at Vegas World sometime in 1993 or 1994. The witness said he was employed as a poker dealer when the younger Jones told him that he was looking for a gun. Hunt turned over the Davis .380 to his friend, but testified that he couldn't remember if he'd given it to him as a gift or was paid for it. The witness added that he'd registered the firearm with the police department, but didn't know whether Bobby Junior had changed the registration.

When he was shown the weapon, Hunt said that it was the same gun, but wasn't in the same shape as the last time he saw it. "It looks older, scratched up," he observed. Hunt said the weapon still had the chrome plating he remembered and thought it had the same grips, but it had had a clip when he turned it over to young Bobby.

A juror asked Hunt whether his friend had told him why he wanted a gun, and Hunt replied that he'd merely said he was having problems. Young Bobby was a good friend and "I would have done anything if he wanted," the witness explained in slightly fractured syntax.

Roger also showed the Davis .380 to Suzanne Anton, who said she had seen it in her mother's dresser drawer. She said that it belonged to her mother, and mistakenly stated that the last time she'd seen it was when police came with a warrant and took it away. A .380 is basically a short version of a 9mm, and it could be easy for someone who isn't expert in such matters to mistake one for the other. Suzanne said that there were actually two guns at the house, a little silver one and a bigger one. "I don't like guns. I don't touch them," she said. "I could care less to really look at them."

Asked about the celebration at the MGM, Suzanne replied that she didn't remember if she'd gambled that night. "We don't gamble," she said. "We play bingo." The witness claimed that her mother was flush with money because she'd had a lucky streak playing bingo at Jerry's Nugget. Cheryl had won $100 one night, and $1,000 the next night, Suzanne said.

Bobby Junior's former girlfriend, Lee Sue Steininger, testified that he'd swapped the pistol to his father for a shotgun when they drove to Point Roberts in Washington state to visit a relative. To reach Point Roberts, they'd had to drive around Boundary Bay through a portion of British Columbia, and they weren't permitted to carry a handgun in Canada. So Bobby told her he'd made the swap with his father because it was okay to carry a shotgun during the Canadian leg of the journey. She said she'd seen both Bobbys, father and son, with the Davis .380 at different times.

When Bobby Junior was called to testify, he told the jury that when he first began to date Lee Sue, some of her relatives threatened to shoot him, so he got the gun from his friend. "You're not a violent type of person, are you?"

Roger asked. "I had one DWI [driving while intoxicated] before I quit drinking, probably back in '84 or '83, but that's all," the witness replied. "Nothing with any violence?" the prosecutor persisted. "No," Bobby Junior said.

The thirty-eight-year-old witness testified that he'd kept the pistol in his car after obtaining it from Hunt, because he was worried about problems developing while he was driving to and from work. "They knew where I worked, they knew where I lived, and that was the original purpose," he said. Bobby Junior said that when he and Lee Sue started living together, that solved the problem with her family, and he lost track of the gun. He declared that he hadn't sold the gun, he hadn't tossed it in the desert, hadn't killed Bruce Weinstein, and hadn't given the weapon to Amy DeChant.

Quite a few people, the witness said, knew that he kept the gun in his car, "an old beat-up wreck" that was eventually sold to a junkyard for scrap before he moved to New Mexico. He didn't say that the pistol had been in the car at that time, just that the vehicle was the last place he remembered seeing it. In reply to another question from Roger, Bobby Junior conceded that it was also possible he could have given the gun to his father.

The younger Jones said that he sold fireworks for a while in New Mexico, then worked at several casino jobs. While he and his girlfriend were living in Rio Rancho a few miles north of Albuquerque, he taught her to deal poker. She quit her job as a waitress, and began working as a poker dealer, then learned how to deal blackjack. One night in July 1996, while Lee Sue was in California and he was home alone, his father telephoned him from Grants, a city approximately halfway between Albuquerque and the Arizona state border, and asked for a ride. Bobby Junior testified that he drove to Grants and picked up his father, who was carrying a little duffel bag, and said he was broke and needed money. Bobby Senior stayed only a day or two, then returned about a month later.

Bobby Junior told the panel that the last time he'd seen his father was about two weeks before the grand jury proceeding while Bobby Senior and Cheryl were gambling at a casino in Fort McDowell, Arizona. The witness said he was staying with his friend Richie Reyes while he was back in town for the grand jury proceeding.

Alan Bady testified about turning the older Bobby Jones in to the police, said he had seen him with handguns at the house on North 19th Street, and described the day in late July when his girlfriend's stepfather had come home with the huge stack of $100 bills. Bady said he remembered the approximate date because his birthday was July 26 and it was around that time. The bills were "kind of folded over, folded in half," he said.

The twenty-nine-year-old witness confirmed that he was in custody at the time of the grand jury hearing for violating probation after conviction on a drug charge, and for child abuse and neglect. He added that he'd lived at the Jones house three different times, but never for more than a few months altogether. "I tried to stay on my feet, but when I couldn't do it, they helped me out," he said.

Bady described his former hosts, Bobby and Cheryl, as poker-mad. "Poker tournaments. They could play poker every night, sir," he told the prosecutor. Bady said the couple had gold and fancy silk clothes, but he'd never seen them with a large amount of money until the day in late July when Bobby came home with the $100 bills.

Roger showed the witness the Davis Model P-380 automatic, and Bady agreed that it looked like a handgun he'd seen at the Jones house. But he did a bit of verbal dancing around, and wouldn't say directly that it was definitely the same firearm. "I believe a gun is a gun," he said.

Michael Anthony Lucarelli testified about his relationship with Amy, his work for DeChant & Company, and the
half-baked proposal to try shaking Bruce down by posing
as a cop and threatening an arrest. The witness said that
he'd suggested the shakedown during a period when he was
drinking heavily, but claimed that it was all a big joke and
hadn't gone over well with Amy. "She told me to stay away
from this crazy guy [Bruce]," Lucarelli testified. "I never
even met the man."

Lucarelli said he finally broke off his contact with Amy
because his wife, Katie, didn't like her and suspected that
they were carrying on an affair. "Katie didn't trust her,
didn't like her," he stated. "Katie always said I was being
used, which in effect I was, with the business and all
that . . ." Lucarelli said he finally broke off all contact with
Amy, but that even after he'd quit calling, she surprised
him with a visit in June 1996, a couple of weeks before the
fateful July Fourth weekend.

He was working in sales for a Nissan dealer one rainy
day, when Amy suddenly drove up to the offices looking
for him. It had been about four months since they'd last
talked, and he hadn't even realized that she knew where he
was working. Lucarelli stood outside in the rain talking
with her for a few minutes. Amy looked as gloomy as the
nasty, drizzly weather and he asked her what was wrong.
She said she was having trouble with Bruce.

"Why don't you just leave him?" Lucarelli asked.

"Well, I have a plan to leave him," she replied.

Roger turned the questioning to Amy's aggressive quest
for money, and Lucarelli said, "She was smart. She was
good-business–minded, real money-hungry. She knew how
to handle a dollar, but pretty much, that was her whole life,
was money. All she ever used to say is, 'I want to retire. I

want to retire.' " Amy was forty-six at that time.

The grand jury also listened to testimony from other former boyfriends of Amy's, including Keith Leroy Bower, the poker room supervisor she'd dated and dumped, then called on for help after Bruce disappeared. Bower briefly described his relationship with Amy, and said that she'd stayed in touch with him after leaving the second time. Their last contact had been on a Saturday night a couple of weeks earlier, when she'd telephoned him at work and asked about his impending grand jury appearance.

Bower said he didn't know where Amy had been calling from, but she knew all about the grand jury being convened to hear evidence in the case. He said he'd told her he had been subpoenaed, ". . . and, I mean, I didn't know why I was going to the grand jury, but I have no other problems in my life besides her." The witness added that Amy was smart enough to know that if he'd received a grand jury subpoena, it probably involved her.

Bower had telephoned Amy's lawyer, Daniel Albregts, after talking with her to find out if he needed an attorney to accompany him to the grand jury proceeding. He was told that Albregts couldn't represent him because he was already Amy's lawyer, and that witnesses in grand jury proceedings couldn't take attorneys with them anyway. Bower added that Amy had promised to take care of the costs if Albregts thought he needed an attorney to appear with him.

"She said that she would pay for it?" Roger asked. "For his time," Bower said. "For Mr. Albregts to come down?" the prosecutor persisted. "To come down with me if I needed an attorney," Bower confirmed.

This brief exchange served as an unsettling reminder of Amy's chronic ability to drag her friends into her troubles, legal and otherwise.

Roger suddenly switched the direction of questioning to

a disturbing new tack: "You weren't involved in the killing of Bruce Weinstein, were you?" he asked.

"No, sir, I was not," the startled witness responded.

"Where were you on July 5, 1996?" Roger demanded.

"Is that a Friday?" Bower asked.

Roger confirmed that it was.

"I was at work, I hope, between the hours—" Bower started over. "I work from 6 o'clock at night to 2 o'clock in the morning at Stateline, Nevada. I have witnesses," he declared. The prosecutor asked which casino he worked at, and who his supervisor was. Bower said he worked at the Primadonna Resorts, named his supervisor, and again declared: "I have witnesses." Bower said that he regularly picked up fellow employes at about 4 p.m. and they drove to work in Stateline, where they were served dinner by the casino. Amy's longtime friend could provide witnesses showing that he'd been with them from 4 p.m. to 3 a.m. on the night of the murder.

In response to another question by the Chief Deputy DA, the witness conceded that he still had feelings for Amy, but when asked if he loved her, he said he didn't know.

"Do you care for her?" Roger asked.

"I care for her, yes," Bower agreed. "Before, when I made this, I would have told you, yes, I was very much in love with her. After I lived with her for a few months, I can't be sure anymore," he said. Then he blurted out: "She's kind of a nasty woman."

Roger quickly broke in and instructed the jurors to disregard the unsolicited observation about Amy's character. The witness skated on the edge of talking out of turn once more a few minutes later when one of the jurors asked if he had been concerned about Amy's safety after she'd told him the story about being threatened by Bruce's killers. "Well, I think she's a little crazy, because the day we traveled around, it's like, if she sees a car behind us, it's like, 'They're following us,' " he replied. "They weren't following us, so, you know, until something happens, you have to show me."

Bower admitted that he was concerned for Amy, but asked: "What are you going to do? She doesn't want to go to the cops. You know, it's her life. You have to live with your decisions. I have to live with my decisions," he said. "I kept telling her to go to the police, and she kept saying, 'No.' "

Bruce's ex-wife, Elizabeth Rose Tuch, was sworn in, told the jury she lived in Arcadia, California, and then began recounting her relationship with the murdered man. Roger asked if Bruce had flashed his money around when they were out in public, and she replied: "No, he was always claiming poverty. He was always saying that he lost. You know, if a game was playing or whatever, he lost. He lost, he lost."

The Chief Deputy DA asked if people who hadn't known Bruce would likely know that he had a lot of money because of his habits or the way he "displayed things." She replied that people who'd known him probably would, because they would also have known that he was one of the biggest bookmakers in the city.

Roger hadn't asked about people who already knew Bruce. He wanted to know if Bruce's behavior in public would have been likely to tip off strangers that he had a lot of money, so he tried again. "But to an ordinary person that did not know him, was Mr. Weinstein flashy with his jewelry?"

"Could be," the witness replied. "When we were married he had a convertible Mercedes, so he drove a nice car. He wore a gold watch and a gold necklace, but— So people would think he was well-to-do, or he was okay," she said.

Roger observed that she had previously stated that Bruce provided about $10,000 to $13,000 for monthly living expenses, and asked if, other than that, he gave her much money. "No, no," she started. "Bruce—I'm not gonna sugarcoat this here. He was a sonofabitch! That's why I divorced him. No, he wouldn't," she said. If she'd wanted money for the store or something and he was in a bad mood, he would be nasty, but eventually forked over whatever she needed, the witness said. "Everything with him was like pulling teeth." Mrs. Tuch agreed that Bruce bought extravagant items for her, but she said it was always a fight. "It was, yeah, he bought me a nice car. I had a lovely diamond ring, diamond necklace, diamond bracelet, but I didn't come by them easy. It wasn't a gracious gift."

The witness testified that, before she'd met her ex-husband, "he was diagnosed with manic depression, or bipolar disorder," and he had severe mood swings. She recounted the time that he'd struck her, and what she claimed was emotionally abusive behavior. And she told about cleaning out their safety deposit box when she left him.

When questioning turned to Amy, the witness described the relationship the two women developed during their telephone discussions about Jaclyn and about their mutual experiences with Bruce. She said they had talked about once a month, and it was sometimes easier to deal with Amy than with Bruce. Roger asked if it would be fair to characterize her feelings toward Bruce "as disenchanted, or perhaps bitter?"

"Yes, yes, he was," the witness replied in a somewhat slewed response. "It was not easy being married to him. It was not easy being divorced from him." The ex-wife agreed that she shared those feelings with Amy, who had indicated having some of the same difficulties with Bruce. Mrs. Tuch said they'd developed somewhat of a bond because of their mutual experience. One time, when Amy had mentioned that she just walked away when Bruce was moody, Elizabeth told her, "You must be a saint."

Even though Amy had complained about Bruce's treatment, he'd thought his new girlfriend was great, the witness testified. "He said if she could have had kids, he would have married her," Mrs. Tuch stated. But, she said, he continued to show an interest in her own life, and if she had wanted him back, she believed he would have been interested.

The witness said she'd called the house in Las Vegas after learning that Bruce was missing, and Amy told her she had about $15,000 in expenses, including all the phone bills for the business and other household accounts that were in her name. So she'd told Amy to search the house, because Bruce always kept money handy. She directed her to look under the carpets and check his suit pockets, because he always had money in the house.

"Do you remember specifically telling her to check under the carpets?" Roger asked.

"I'm guilty of that," the witness replied. "I did it. I told her to do that. Yeah."

Yohan Lowie, who'd constructed Bruce's custom-built home, was called to testify before the panel about the crackling noises he'd heard on July 5, 1996, about security features at the house, and about other matters. Lowie explained that he had been born in Israel and, while serving in the army there, was in charge of the Division for Special Light Arms, which included handguns with silencers, special sniping systems, and small shoulder-propelled missiles for special operations.

Roger asked Lowie if he had "a special ear for ammunition and gunshots" as a result of his training and expe-

rience with firearms that enabled him to distinguish
different types. "I should," the witness responded. "I was
trained for it—to distinguish between various weapon gunshots." Even the experts can make an occasional mistake,
however, and Lowie conceded that, although the popping
noises outside Bruce's house had initially sounded like gunshots, he'd wanted to believe they were firecrackers. It went
unsaid, but the quiet little community on the outskirts of
Las Vegas wasn't Israel in wartime and there seemed to be
no reason anyone would be shooting off firearms.

Roger asked if, in retrospect, Lowie had an opinion
about whether or not the noises he heard were a high-
caliber popping or low-caliber gunshots.

"With all honesty, I was thinking as soon as I heard the
noises: 'Are those shots?' " he replied. "And I wanted to
believe, or thought it to be firecrackers. But for the noise,
if I had to make an assumption of what caliber weapon
would shot [sic] a noise like that, it would be medium to
small caliber." Lowie further explained that anything under
22 to 9 logo, including .380 automatics, 760 Berlinettis,
and certain quiet ammunition were low caliber.

Scientific aspects of the investigation, specifically tests
with DNA and serology and blood analysis, were the focus
of testimony by David Welch, a criminalist with twenty
years' experience as a forensic chemist for the Las Vegas
Metro Police Department. At the time of his testimony he
had been working with DNA for three years, and provided
details about some of the laboratory tests and comparisons
made with blood and DNA samples linked to the case.
Some of the work was carried out in the police laboratory,
and other especially sophisticated DNA testing was conducted at Cellmark Diagnostics in Maryland.

The tests included work with the blood samples provided
by Bruce's parents; samples of muscle tissue, hair, and

bone taken from the remains; blood from the mattress and foam sheet, a sandal with pink and green straps; suspicious-looking stains on a chunk cut from the beige carpeting in the house on Castle Vista Court; and a stained white towel, a tan cloth, a fluid sample, and a swab, all taken from the DeChant & Company Aerostar work van. The sheet of foam taken from under the mattress of Bruce's bed was heavily soaked with human blood, and the mattress itself had a smaller amount on it. The carpeting, and the towel and tan cloth taken from the van, also tested positive, but the swab and the sandal tested negative, Welch told the rapt jurors.

During testimony by Dr. Jordan, the pathologist was asked by a juror if, based on the limited remains he had to work with, Bruce might have suffered more than one gun-shot wound. "None that I saw," Jordan replied. "There could have possibly been more than one if the bullet had passed through soft tissue and didn't leave any tell-tale marks on the bone. We wouldn't have ever found it."

Alford B. Leavitt, a larger-than-life character and hard-boiled former Metro homicide detective who had been called from retirement in Idaho to testify about organized crime killings in Las Vegas—one of his specialties—may have been the most compelling of the grand jury witnesses. Leavitt had joined the former Clark County Sheriff's Department in 1963, a full decade before the merger with the Las Vegas city police, and, during more than twenty-three years with the homicide division, investigated 466 murders. He estimated that about a dozen were directly linked to organized crime.

A big 265-pound man with a strong, commanding voice and an easy comfort on the witness chair that comes with experience, the retired homicide investigator scoffed at Amy's preposterous yarn about Bruce being the victim of a Mob hit. "You know, some people will tell you that organized crime is two or more people conspiring to commit a murder or to commit a crime," he declared after briefly reviewing Amy's statement. "If there's organized crime involved in this, it's got to be Amy or one of her boyfriends involved . . . If it was organized crime from New York or Chicago—Mob, you know—she would have never still been alive. If they went in the house with her in there, they would have killed her. She never would have stood a prayer."

The witness labeled Amy's reputed gentle handling after she was pulled from the shower as "a fairy tale." Then he launched into a grisly recitation of some of the organized crime murders he'd investigated, taking the jurors along with him on a dark journey through the sewers of the city while drawing a verbal portrait of violent death, Las Vegas–style.

Leavitt told the jurors that if real mobsters were planning a hit they would most likely have planned the house invasion for a time when Amy wasn't home, because she would have had nothing to do with the motive for killing Bruce. But if they had gone inside and killed him and found her there, they would kill her too, because she would have been a witness.

The latest round of grand jury testimony accomplished its purpose, pulling the remaining threads of the investigation together and wrapping Amy DeChant and Bobby Jones tightly up inside a cocoon of guilt. On September 12, more than fourteen months after Bruce vanished from his home, the Clark County Grand Jury returned indictments to Chief Judge Myron E. Leavitt accusing Amy and Bobby of murder and other felonies in connection with the death. Each of the defendants was named on charges of conspiracy to commit robbery and/or murder, murder with use of a deadly weapon, and robbery with use of a deadly weapon. Bobby was also charged with an additional count of accessory to murder.

Warrants were sworn out for their arrests, and after another *America's Most Wanted* program was broadcast, a tipster telephoned information about Bobby's whereabouts to Metro police. The information was immediately passed on to the Las Vegas Metro Police–FBI Fugitive Task Force. A Task Force officer telephoned police in Gallup, New Mexico, and Bobby was taken into custody by a team of law enforcement officers. He was returned to Las Vegas and locked in the Clark County Detention Center without bail to await trial. Deputy Special Public Defender Kristina Wildeveld was appointed to represent the Las Vegas grandfather. In November, in the Eighth District Court, he entered a formal plea of not guilty to all charges filed against him.

Chief Deputy DA Roger offered Amy a chance through her attorney to turn herself in, and gave her a few days to comply. When she failed to show up by the deadline, he obtained a warrant for her arrest. Once more, Amy was on the run.

CHAPTER TWELVE

JACKPOT

"A man that doeth violence to the blood of any
person shall flee to the pit; let no man stay him."
PROVERBS 28:17

Host John Walsh and his colleagues at *America's Most
Wanted* had been giving Bobby Jones nightmares, and once
he was in custody, they turned their attention to Amy De-
Chant, whom everybody involved with the Bruce Weinstein
investigation believed was the brains behind the murder.
Police and prosecutors were convinced that, if Amy hadn't
actually pulled the trigger, she was the person who'd set
up the slaying.

On January 3, 1998, approximately eighteen months after she went on the run again, the syndicated television
program broadcast a third segment about Bruce's murder,
and this time they focused on the search for Amy.

Within minutes after the profile was broadcast, the
switchboards at *AMW*'s 1-800–CRIME-TV hotline, and at
the St. Lucie County Sheriff's Department on Florida's
Gold Coast, began lighting up with calls. The callers all
passed on basically the same message: A woman who
looked just like Amy DeChant was living at the Sunnier

Palms Nudist Park on Okeechobee Road a few miles west of the city of Fort Pierce. She called herself "Sandy Wade."

Once more, she was hiding in plain sight, living in a trailer home with another boyfriend, and helping out part-time with office work at the nudist park. During some of her free hours at Sunnier Palms, she alarmed local admirers by cutting firewood with a power saw—in the nude, of course.

While hiding out in south Florida, Amy had been her usual busy self, maintaining an industrious work schedule, driving back and forth between the Sunshine State and New Jersey, and charming a succession of admirers and live-in boyfriends she met on the job or while hanging around Sunnier Palms and local watering holes. She attended a bartending school in West Palm Beach, and trained for about a week at the Out Of Bounds Steak and Grill in Fort Pierce, a restaurant and bar on the ocean side of U.S. Highway 1 that hugs the Atlantic coastline all the way from Key West north into Georgia.

The Out Of Bounds is sandwiched between an ABC Liquor Store and a mini–shopping center that are part of a splatter of retail stores, restaurants and other business buildings that stretch almost non-stop along both sides of the highway, except for occasional patches of scrub weeds and sabal palms. Amy discovered the steakhouse almost as soon as she got into town, and she fit right into the crowd. Most of the men she chatted up liked her, but some of the women were more stand-offish. She was too perky and sweet to be real.

Amy also tended bar for a while at the Rocking Horse American Night Club in Stuart, another small Gold Coast town about twenty miles south of Fort Pierce in adjoining Martin County, and sometimes made the rounds at the St. Lucie Draft House in Port St. Lucie. For someone who was employed as a bartender and doing part-time office work at a nudist camp, the woman known by her south Florida friends as Sandy Wade had an awful lot of cash on hand. At her urging, some of her new male friends helped her convert some of the currency into money orders.

Donald Esper, the boyfriend whose trailer home she'd shared at the camp, was unaware that she was a fugitive from murder charges in Nevada, and had asked her to attend a convention with him in Las Vegas. She declined. She was a mysterious woman who was obviously harboring deep secrets. One day, after Amy asked Esper to keep a can with $10,000 in a false bottom for her, he asked what was going on. "You're better off not knowing what I did," she replied.

Somehow, Amy learned of the planned *AMW* broadcast a few days before the show was aired, and cleared out of Sunnier Palms. She dressed, tossed some additional clothes, grooming aids, and a few other treasures into a couple of bags, and headed out the door to her Cadillac. "Things are hot," she told her boyfriend. "I can't tell you why, but I gotta go. I'm out of here."

When the FBI showed up at the nudist camp a couple of days later, there was no sign of the outrageously unconventional charmer. Sandy/Amy was on the run again. Esper also moved out of the camp and relocated in a mobile home in Trenton, Michigan. Time was rapidly running out for his sweetheart from Sunnier Palms.

Near the end of January, less than one month after Amy was profiled on the television program, tipsters called the *AMW* hotline and contacted the St. Lucie County Sheriff's Department with information that the fugitive was back in town. A sergeant assigned to the St. Lucie County Jail was tipped off by an outside acquaintance that the woman known as Sandy Wade had slipped back into the county or was about to return. The corrections officer relayed the information to Derrick Peterson, a young investigator who had recently left Road Patrol and joined the Detective Bureau. The confidential informant—"CI" in police terminology—was cagey and didn't want his name revealed. So Peterson gave his telephone number to the corrections officer and asked him to pass it along to the CI and ask him to call.

Instead of contacting Peterson, the cautious informant talked again to the corrections officer, and left a telephone number. The sergeant passed the number on to another detective, Charles Scavuzzo, who immediately telephoned the wary tipster and began coaxing information out of him. After a few moments of hemming and hawing, the CI finally got to the point. He wasn't bothered by the idea of informing on Amy, he just wanted to make sure he got the reward that *America's Most Wanted* had said was being offered for her arrest.

An investigator for more than seven years, first with the Narcotics Unit, then with the Detective Bureau, Scavuzzo advised the tipster to give him the information about Amy's whereabouts, and to deal with the reward later. The detective wasn't familiar with the details of the reward at that time, but he was eager to move quickly and make an arrest before the elusive fugitive slipped away again. Take the money matters up with the people offering the reward, he advised.

The contact reluctantly agreed, and provided a general description of the fugitive's appearance and of her car. The tipster said that the woman he knew as "Sandy" was driving a white Cadillac and could be found in nearby Port St. Lucie at the home of a local small businessman named Joe Kosa, who operated a janitorial service. The CI said that Sandy had been to his house and had met with him on prior

occasions before she left town. She'd just driven back to
St. Lucie County the previous evening from Bayville, near
the central New Jersey shore.

After concluding his talk with the informant, Scavuzzo
contacted *America's Most Wanted* to verify the information,
and arranged for his contact there to fax a photo of the
fugitive and additional data to him at the sheriff's department. Then he telephoned the local FBI office and asked
to speak to the agent, whom sources at *AMW* said was
heading the area search for Amy. An office secretary told
Scavuzzo that the agent was busy on the telephone. The
police detective explained that he had valuable information
about a fugitive and suggested that she interrupt the agent,
but she refused.

So Scavuzzo went to his boss, Captain Robert Miller,
and to Sergeant Diane M. Thompson with the information.
Miller, a tall, slim, handsome man with wavy salt-and-
pepper hair, who looks a bit like a young Hal Lindsey on
the old "Barney Miller" television show, was head of the
Criminal Investigations Division—CID. CID Sergeant
Thompson, who was assigned to Major Crimes, is also
slim, bright-eyed, experienced, and a fast read. The captain
and the sergeant called a quick war council and decided to
act immediately. Aware that the fugitive had just managed
to elude authorities only a couple of weeks earlier when
she fled the nudist camp, they were determined to see to it
that she didn't repeat the performance.

Miller, Scavuzzo, Peterson, Thompson, and a couple of
uniformed officers piled into three unmarked cars and drove
away from the sheriff's department headquarters, heading
for the Kosa home at 131 Solaz Avenue in Port St. Lucie.
The little fleet of plain cars silently pulled to a stop several
yards from the house a few minutes later, and placed it

under surveillance. It was about 8 o'clock Wednesday morning, January 28.

Kosa lived in a nice house in a quiet, pleasant neighborhood that was well isolated from the roar of traffic and gritty exhaust fumes of cars and trucks on the nearby highways. The single-story, two-bedroom residence was Spanish-style beige stucco with a robust-looking palm tree near the entrance, a well-manicured lawn and a large, well-shaded front porch with furniture. A white Cadillac and a van were parked in front, both of late 1980s vintage. Scavuzzo made a quick scan of the tag numbers provided by the CI. The Cadillac's were a perfect match.

About five minutes after Captain Miller and his crew set up the stake-out, a plain blue Toyota pickup truck stopped in front of the house, and a sturdy middle-aged man with white hair, a neatly trimmed goatee, and a mustache stepped outside. He didn't seem to be surprised to see the waiting police posse and behaved as if he already knew what was going on. He identified himself as Joe Kosa, and said the house belonged to him. Scavuzzo asked if there was a woman in the house, and Kosa confirmed that there was. "Is her name Amy DeChant?" the detective asked. "No, it's Sandy," Kosa replied.

Kosa readily consented to permit the stake-out team to enter the house, and as the businessman opened a side door, Scavuzzo, Miller, and their colleagues saw a drowsy-appearing woman standing in the kitchen wearing a bathrobe and a pair of fuzzy flip-flops. She looked surprised to see them, and when Scavuzzo asked for her name, she stammered. She said her first name was Sandy, but seemed to be having special difficulty remembering her last name, so the burly detective suggested that she start over and try again. That brought a shrug of her shoulders and an admission that she was Amy DeChant. Then she held out her arms and Thompson snapped a pair of handcuffs on her wrists. "How did you catch me? How did you find me?" the shackled woman repeatedly asked.

It was an easy collar. None of the officers had drawn their service pistols, before entering the house or while making the arrest. Amy was standing only a few feet away when Kosa opened the door, and she didn't try to run or to resist. After Sergeant Thompson patted her down and the officers took a quick look around the kitchen, Scavuzzo ordered her to sit in a plain straight-backed chair with no soft cushions, folds of material, or other handy hiding places.

Amy wasn't dressed for traveling, so the arrest team told her to pick an outfit from a suitcase full of clothes she had with her and change in the bathroom. The prisoner made her selections, including a pair of stretch pants and a sweatshirt with a football logo from Superbowl XXXI in New Orleans on the front. Thompson carefully checked the clothing for weapons or any other forbidden materials, then inspected the bathroom, rummaging through the medicine cabinet and peering behind the shower curtains. At last she unlocked the cuffs, ushered the prisoner inside, and left the door open a crack while she stood watch just outside.

While the prisoner was changing clothes, Scavuzzo made a telephone call to the local FBI office and advised the agent in charge of the search for Amy that she was in custody. The sheriff's detective later recalled with some glee that the agent was upset and complained that the local officers weren't playing fair. Local FBI officers had been gathering information on Amy's whereabouts for six months, barely missed capturing her at Sunnier Palms, and most recently were investigating reports that she was downstate in the Homestead area south of Miami. The FBI hadn't previously shared the information about Amy with St. Lucie County sheriff's officers.

Kosa sat at his kitchen table silently watching the proceedings while Amy was placed under arrest, allowed to dress, handcuffed again, then led outside and helped into a marked patrol unit summoned to transport her to sheriff's department headquarters. She was still asking the officers how they had caught up with her. The Cadillac and the heavily loaded van were driven onto flatbed trucks and hauled back to the headquarters on Midway Road, then logged into the auto pound to be searched later. Police also confiscated a couple of firearms from Kosa's house just to make sure they had no bearing on the case. The handguns had nothing to do with Amy, and they were returned to the owner a short time later.

Kosa agreed to follow the arresting officers back to headquarters, where he was led into an interrogation room for questioning. Captain Miller and Detective Scavuzzo had already virtually eliminated him as a willing accomplice, and the interview confirmed their initial conclusions. The St. Lucie County deputies learned that the businessman had tried the previous day to notify the FBI agent that Amy was in Fort Pierce, and was shunted aside. The sheriff's officers later learned that she had been on her way to Homestead when she stopped off in St. Lucie County.

When Kosa was confronted by the St. Lucie County Sheriff's Department officers early Wednesday morning, he was returning from their headquarters on Midway Road after notifying authorities with the Crime Stoppers program that the woman profiled on *AMW* was at his house. Informing on his houseguest wasn't a pleasant task. The pair had had a good time together after meeting at the Out Of Bounds steakhouse, talking, joking and giggling. "I mean," Kosa later remarked, "it makes a gentleman feel like he's wanted." Amy was good company when she wasn't scheming—and sometimes when she was hip-deep in a conspiracy of some kind or another, she was even better. She knew how to play the game of love, and how to keep a romantic relationship alive with come-hither promises and a smattering of sexual intrigue.

A pair of FBI men, including the agent Scavuzzo had tried to talk with, were waiting when the sheriff's department officers walked into the Criminal Investigations Division offices. They also talked with Kosa and asked why he hadn't told them about Amy being at his house. He replied that he'd tried to, but they wouldn't listen. The horse was already out of the barn. A bunch of small-town cops had beaten the FBI to the punch, and the woman agents had been seeking for more than six months was already in custody.

Amy was taken to a separate interview room for interrogation by Scavuzzo and Thompson, but she said she didn't want to talk about the case against her and wanted to consult an attorney. They didn't have any local charges against her, but they had contacted their brother officers with the Homicide Unit at Las Vegas Metro and Bigham was already making arrangements to fly to Florida. Amy had towed the Cadillac to Port St. Lucie with the van, and both vehicles were stuffed full of things, the Florida cops told Bigham. "You gotta come and take a look at this," they urged. The sheriff's officers also prepared affidavits to file with the local St. Lucie County courts seeking search warrants for the vehicles and for Amy's suitcases and other personal property.

The prisoner was excessively polite and apologized because she wasn't being more helpful. Then, while Scavuzzo and Thompson were trying to gather basic information for the arrest warrant and other documentation, she volunteered a string of observations and remarks. It was difficult for her to keep her mouth closed very long. She claimed that she had been working with an acting guild while traveling around the country.

Sergeant Thompson noticed that the animated woman with the reddish-brown hair and sparkling blue eyes seemed to enjoy her dark celebrity. She grinned steadily from the time she first sat down for the interrogation to the time she was told they were through with her. Amy chatted easily about her notoriety and about the nickname she'd acquired back home in Nevada as "the Black Widow of Las Vegas." She was clearly disappointed when Thompson and Scavuzzo said in response to one of her questions that it had taken only about an hour to run her down. She acted like her feelings were hurt.

Amy wanted to talk, but she didn't want to dig a deeper hole for herself, so she couched much of her conversation in theoretical terms. She started sentences with words and phrases such as "Hypothetically speaking," and "If I had done . . ." It was a ploy that suspects frequently use to deal with police when they are looking for information from interrogators and attempting to control the direction of the questioning without making any admissions.

As she had earlier when talking with Wysocki, Amy painted herself as the victim in the whole affair. She repeated the routine about being threatened and chased by mobsters. Scavuzzo and Thompson finally finished with the forms, and ended the conversation.

Amy was led outside, still handcuffed, helped into a marked car, and driven approximately five miles to the St. Lucie County Jail on Rock Road and Orange Avenue. Local newspaper and television reporters and photographers were waiting at the jail when the police car pulled up with the prisoner inside. The arrest of the woman so recently profiled on *America's Most Wanted* and identified as "the Black Widow of Las Vegas" was big news in the quiet little oceanside community.

With Scavuzzo on one side of her and Sergeant Thompson on the other, Amy was led through the jam of newshounds, and taken inside. She was having a bad hair day, and her rowdy swirl of frizzy, shoulder-length hair looked like a dried-out dust mop. For once, she kept her mouth closed, refusing to respond to shouted questions. Inside the jail the forty-nine-year-old woman was quickly processed. She was directed to stand in front of a monitoring screen with a built-in camera that snapped a full-face frontal shot, then fed the picture directly into the computer. No profiles were taken. She was given a shower, issued a pair of baggy, bright-orange scrubs and rubber slides, then locked in a cell in the felony dormitory with another woman prisoner. During the rest of her stay at the jail, Amy would eat and spend all of her free time in the dormitory with other inmates.

When the news of Amy's arrest hit Las Vegas, Chief Deputy DA Roger told news reporters that he was hopeful she could be extradited quickly so that she and Bobby Jones could be put on trial together. Bobby's first-degree-murder trial had been slated to begin the following week before Eighth Judicial District Court Judge John S. McGroarty, but the day Amy drove back to Florida from New Jersey, the defendant requested a continuance and the proceeding was rescheduled for March 9. Now it appeared that Bobby's day in court might be rescheduled even further in the future so that he and Amy could be put on trial in a joint proceeding.

Albregts was less forthcoming when reporters asked him about the arrest. He said that Amy had been in touch and he would begin preparing her defense. "It would be premature to say anything else," he told the *SUN*.

Bigham and his new partner on the case, Dave Messinar,

flew into Fort Lauderdale early Thursday, and drove a rented car up I-95 to St. Lucie County. Immediately after their arrival, they got down to the business of searching the Cadillac and the van. The vehicles, some suitcases, and other property confiscated at the Kosa home yielded a storehouse of promising evidence, including $2,000 in cash and money orders. The money orders were all in $100 increments, and were stuffed in the false bottom of a Jiffy Pop can along with the currency.

Detective Scavuzzo, Sergeant George Miller from the Crime Scene Division, and a lieutenant joined the Las Vegas officers in the search of the vehicles and suitcase. Among the most intriguing discoveries were several wigs, and a briefcase filled with sunglasses, conventional eyeglasses, cosmetics, creams, powders, stage makeup and special pads used in the acting profession to change facial contours. Written directions were included with the material, explaining how to use makeup and pads to age someone. With the right amount of effort and practice, Amy could have made herself appear to be seventy years old or older. The discovery brought her unsolicited remarks about belonging to an acting guild into sharp focus. She had obviously known that police would find her stash of wigs and stage makeup. A short list of telephone numbers, including numbers for Oprah Winfrey and a couple of other television talk shows, was also found.

Other discoveries included brand-new machines and cans of paint for the parking-lot-striping business, a ledger with what appeared to be coded numbers relating to stock purchases, a laptop computer, and safety deposit keys for several different locations and identities. One of the keys was for a box in Toms River, New Jersey, a community along the Garden State Parkway in Ocean County where Scavuzzo grew up. Toms River is across the state, southwest of the New Brunswick area where Amy spent many of her earlier years, and where her brother Mickey lived and worked. It's also the town that Claudia McClure recalled forwarding mail to.

Bigham and Messinar had barely returned to Fort Lauderdale after completing the search of the vehicles, before Amy sprung a big surprise. She waived extradition and agreed to return to Las Vegas without the fuss of a prolonged legal proceeding in the St. Lucie County courts or the issuing of a governor's warrant.

The Las Vegas officers were taken completely off-guard. When they boarded a jet at McCarran International Airport they were carrying notebooks and expecting to conduct searches of a couple of vehicles in a police impound yard, to exchange information with officers in St. Lucie County, and perhaps talk to a few other people. They didn't even bring their weapons or handcuffs with them—or a female officer. Department regulations say that when it's feasible, women prisoners should be escorted by a female officer. It made good sense, especially so when the prisoner was a tease and a lifelong temptress like Amy DeChant, who had made a career out of capitalizing on her sexual appeal to manipulate men.

When Bigham telephoned his superiors at the Metro Homicide Unit and told them about the surprising new development, he was directed to return Amy to Las Vegas. It wasn't feasible to fly a woman officer all the way to Florida and back as an escort, and no one even mentioned it.

So Bigham called on his new friends in St. Lucie County and asked if they would transport the prisoner to Fort Lauderdale. They agreed, and Sergeant Thompson and Detective Scavuzzo drove Amy downstate. It was a memorable ride. Even though Amy was locked in wrist- and ankle-shackles, she told stories and joked all the way down I-95 to the Fort Lauderdale International Airport. She teased that truckers were going to run them off the road, and helicopters would swoop down from the sky and help her make a break for freedom. She was funny, animated, and behaved as if she loved being in the spotlight.

Before Scavuzzo and Thompson helped her out of the back seat of the patrol car and led her inside the Broward County Sheriff's Department Security Office at the airport, she turned serious. She thanked both officers for being so courteous to her, and tipped them off to the best places to gamble in Las Vegas. She named a couple of casinos which she assured them had the best payoff rates for slot machines. The chatty prisoner also thanked them for her nice treatment at the St. Lucie County Jail. Amy was treated like a celebrity by other inmates, and said she couldn't believe how nice everyone was to a fugitive.

The St. Lucie County officers stood guard over their prisoner in the security office until Bigham and Messinar showed up carrying their luggage and a couple of sacks stuffed with evidence, then turned her over to the Las Vegas cops. A little smirk crossed Amy's face when she saw Bigham, but when he mentioned that he had the laptop and was going to execute a search warrant to find out what kind of information was stored on it she said she wanted to telephone her lawyer. Bigham was hopeful that the laptop could help break the apparent code used to make the entries in the ledger that were believed to be linked to stock investments.

The police officers waited only a few feet away while Amy talked with Albregts in Las Vegas and could easily overhear her side of the conversation. "Well, they want to search the computer," she said. Then there was a pause.

"No, there's nothing on there," she said. "It's basically clean."

When Amy concluded the conversation and hung up the phone, she turned to the detectives and told them she didn't mind if they looked into her computer. Then she gave them her password. Bigham appreciated the courtesy. It saved Clark County taxpayers the expense of hiring a professional hacker to figure it out.

Bigham borrowed a pair of handcuffs from his Florida colleagues, then draped Amy's bright blue suit jacket over her wrists to hide the shackles, and he and his partner led their prisoner onto a waiting jetliner for the flight back to Nevada. As Amy disappeared through the door leading to the waiting jet, she again thanked the St. Lucie County officers for their cordial treatment.

According to the established routine, the officers and their prisoner boarded the aircraft before other passengers and sat in the last row of seats next to the rest rooms. Amy was dressed in the same casual sweater and slacks she'd worn from Kosa's home to the St. Lucie County Jail, but it was plain that the slender woman with the cuffed wrists, crunched on a center seat between two burly men, was a prisoner. The airline stewardesses and other members of the crew knew that a LEO—police and air crew jargon for a working law enforcement officer—was aboard, and it wasn't very long before other people began stealing furtive glances at them after nearby seats filled with passengers.

Amy chatted comfortably with the two detectives about inconsequential matters during the flight. Bigham told her that someone had mailed a flyer to police advertising the parking-lot-striping business, mentioned the trunk full of expensive equipment, and asked if the venture had made any money. Amy shrugged it off. It was just another business idea, but it never really worked out that well, she said. When Amy asked to use the bathroom the detectives got up, discreetly removed her handcuffs, and stood in the gal-

ley area with a couple of stewardesses while she disappeared inside the little cubicle for a few minutes. Neither
of her escorts was armed, but as soon as she emerged from
the rest room, they snapped the cuffs on again and the trio
returned to their seats.

The Las Vegas lawmen weren't able to book a non-stop
flight, and when the aircraft landed in Houston they remained aboard with their prisoner. They wound up sitting
in the stuffy airplane for two hours after mechanics discovered a broken part. It was an uncomfortable wait, but the
detectives decided it was preferable to disembarking and
filling out a new round of paperwork before reboarding and
resuming their flight. It was also safer. Amy wasn't likely
to be able to overpower two husky men without a weapon
of some kind, even if she had wanted to. But if they escorted her inside the terminal, there was always the danger
of some outside interference. So they stayed put, chatting
with the stewardesses and the captain. The pilot and Messinar were both Vietnam veterans, so they exchanged war
stories for a while.

A camera crew from *America's Most Wanted* and other
members of the local media were waiting in the terminal
when Amy and her escorts disembarked at McCarran. Amy
wasn't her usual bubbly, loquacious self. She was talked
out, and when she saw the crunch of media waiting for her,
she peered at Bigham and asked in her most plaintive little-
girl voice: "Do I have to talk to these people?"

"You don't have to talk to anybody," Bigham told her.
Amy dropped her head one time, but only for a moment.
Then she straightened up and marched through the back-
pedaling crowd of reporters and camera crews with her
head up and her mouth closed. They walked all the way to
a special lot set aside at McCarran for county police vehicles, then loaded their passenger inside Bigham's plain car

and drove downtown. When they arrived at the Clark County Detention Center, they drove into the sallyport and the detectives stored their weapons, which they had retrieved, in lockers. Then they helped their handcuffed prisoner out of the car and the plainclothes officers stood before a pair of thick glass doors, showed their IDs, and used a speaker system to further identify themselves as homicide detectives.

Moments later the doors slid open, and they stepped through with their prisoner. The booking area was filled with people sitting on a couple of long wooden benches, or on their feet being processed. Metal bars used to handcuff unruly prisoners when it was necessary were attached to the wall behind the benches. Several other police officers, most in uniform, were filling out papers or otherwise tending to their prisoners.

Amy was directed to sit. She watched silently as Bigham approached a woman seated at a counter behind a shield of bulletproof glass with a speaker system and a small opening at the bottom to pass paperwork through. He signed copies of warrants to show that he had served them on his prisoner, and filled out a declaration of arrest and a temporary custody record. It was all part of the booking routine.

Everyone waits their turn for booking, and prisoners accused of serious felonies are given the same treatment as people brought in for lesser violations of the law. Cops are curious like anyone else, and a few uniformed officers who recognized Bigham and his partner peered at the frowzy-haired woman they'd brought in and asked, "Whatta you got?" "The Black Widow," Bigham replied. Then the detectives and the uniformed cops swapped a few war stories and brought each other up-to-date on what was going on in the local criminal underworld, while waiting with their prisoners.

When it was Amy's turn to be processed, a uniformed officer directed her to stand on a pair of footprints painted on the floor while her photo was taken. Then a female officer patted her down, removed the cuffs, and handed them to Bigham. At that point, Amy belonged to the corrections officers. The job of Bigham and his partner as co-custodians of the prisoner was over. The homicide detectives turned and left her in her new home.

Being booked into a jail or prison can be a humiliating, intimidating ordeal for most men, perhaps even more so for women. Other prisoners waiting their turn may be sobbing, screaming, fighting, chained to the wall, or simply slumping on the bench with a thousand-yard stare like a soldier who's seen too much combat. Often, they're drenched in sweat, from the desert heat outside, or from apprehension over their future. No matter how often the area is cleaned it tends to smell of stale sweat and fear. The experience can be scary and make someone feel like they're drowning, with no rescue in sight.

Bigham and other officers had learned through experience that prisoners may be at their most psychologically vulnerable when they're about to be left alone with their new keepers. Sometimes even the toughest, most streetwise prisoners become so overwhelmed that they break down and are swept by a sudden urge to talk about their crimes.

Amy wasn't one of those people. She had been booked into jails at least a couple of times before, and Bigham was struck by her apparent attitude of nonchalance. If someone told her to sit down, she sat down and waited patiently until she was given a new order. If she was told to place her feet over paint-outlined footsteps, she stepped on the outline. And throughout the several confrontations that the homicide sleuth had had with her, she never once showed any remorse over her boyfriend's grisly death.

A short time after Bigham drove out of the sallyport and headed home to clean up and hit the sack, Amy was given a shower, issued a navy-blue jumpsuit, and assigned to a cell.

Amy was one of the lucky ones. Most of her neighbors in the booking room would be sent to overcrowded first-floor holding pens to spend several hours or more, even a couple of days, until spaces in cells were available for them.

The downtown jail, with all its faults and shortcomings, would be Amy's new home for several months, perhaps far longer, while the often frustratingly tedious process leading up to her trial creaked, sputtered, and whirred into high gear. The misery, the dangers, and the foul odors, which even some corrections officers complained made them so sick that they didn't eat before coming on duty, would be as much a part of her life as the plain concrete, the cement-block walls, the steel bars, and the mind-numbing regimentation.

Her cell, which was shared with one or more other women, and the dormitory just outside would be her world. It was a far cry from the spacious new $675,000 custom-built house just a few miles away on the southwest edge of Las Vegas which she had reigned over as mistress. In her new home, Amy wouldn't be driving off to shop in a shiny late-model Camaro convertible, fussing over marble tables, swimming in a private heated back-yard pool or slipping off to the Orleans to try her luck in poker tournaments. Amy had led police on a madcap chase, and authorities weren't in a mood to give her a chance to flee again. Like Bobby Jones, she was held without bail.

The day after returning his prisoner to Las Vegas, Bigham filled a cardboard box with baseball hats, shirts, and patches carrying the Metro police logo. He dropped the handcuffs inside, and shipped the box to the St. Lucie

County Sheriff's Department in Florida. He and his partner had their own collection of Florida patches and clothes that they'd carried back to Nevada with them.

America's Most Wanted aired one more show about the reputed "Black Widow of Las Vegas." When Amy was run down and picked up in Port St. Lucie, it was a historic occasion for the program. She was the five-hundredth fugitive apprehended after being profiled on the show. On Saturday night, February 28, 1998, ten years after *AMW* debuted, the show broadcast a "500th Capture Special" about Amy. "Our five-hundredth capture was a woman who clearly had nothing to hide," a beaming John Walsh announced to listeners, while slyly alluding to her choice of a nudist camp as a refuge.

Bruce's parents, Mike Wysocki, Metro homicide detectives, and other people involved in the investigation appeared on the Saturday evening show. Peering into the eye of the camera, Wysocki frankly apprised viewers that, after Amy and Bruce became sweethearts, "They would have sex five and six times a day. Amy did everything right."

Sylvia White was equally frank: "She looked like she came out of a whorehouse," the white-haired grandmother said of her eldest son's former girlfriend.

Detective Thomas Thowsen called Amy a "Black Widow," and declared that when she had taken what there was to offer, she moved "on to the next man."

CHAPTER THIRTEEN

RETIRED BEFORE FIFTY

As the opening of the trial drew closer, police and prosecutors had no confession from either Amy or Bobby, and no eyewitnesses—no one who could testify that they had seen Bruce shot to death, carried from his home, and buried on the desert, or who had overheard the defendants scheming to rob and kill the obese gambler.

The state couldn't even say with any certainty which of the defendants was believed to have done the actual shooting. They didn't know if Bobby was pulled into a robbery scheme that resulted in Bruce being shot during a struggle, or if a murder had been planned all along. Although prosecutors had the rusty .380 and witnesses who could testify that it was seen in Bobby's possession, they weren't prepared to prove beyond the shadow of a doubt that it was the murder weapon.

Police and prosecutors nevertheless had weaved together a solidly persuasive web of physical and circumstantial evidence which they were convinced would prove to a jury that Amy DeChant and Bobby Jones were responsible for Bruce Weinstein's death. They firmly believed that they had assembled a sufficient number of facts to show that the defendants killed Bruce for his money with a gun which Bobby was known to have had in his possession.

The state had readied a compelling and forceful account. On the night of July 5, 1996—or perhaps in the pre-dawn darkness of the following morning—Bobby dumped the body in the desert. He later returned to the site with his grandsons during the daylight hours to determine if it was sufficiently concealed. Then he returned once again and moved the body to the extreme northwest part of the county just off Old Alamo Road, rolled it over the edge of the ravine, and covered it with rocks. Bobby would have been familiar with the area because he frequently traveled the roads to Mesquite, where DeChant & Company had carpet-cleaning accounts. Finally he and Amy split the money and cleaned up the blood in the house.

Amy's attorney appeared to be locked into presenting a defense constructed around the basic scenario she had repeatedly drawn for investigators, blaming her lover's murder on mysterious Mob assassins who invaded the home on Castle Vista Court. Amy had told the story too many times to too many people to call for a new deck of cards at that point in the game. Bigham and Thowsen were surprised and puzzled that she stuck with the same tired story about sinister Mob assassins, which had so many obvious holes in it. But throughout her attorney's pre-trial filings, she stubbornly continued to deny and contest anything to the contrary. The state's case, the defense would claim, was based on speculation and innuendo.

Bobby had an opportunity to try and cut a deal for himself by swapping testimony against his former boss for a plea bargain and probable sentence of probation, but never once indicated any interest in such a maneuver. Early in the investigation, Bigham and Thowsen had half-expected Amy to turn on Bobby and try to pin the slaying on him. The homicide cops were jokingly betting that she would concoct a new story claiming that she and her employee had planned to rip Bruce off, but Bobby shot him and messed everything up. Amy was a woman known for using the men in her life as pawns to further her aims, and the detectives figured that betraying Bobby and trying to make him the fall guy wouldn't be out of character.

But the co-suspects, who had become co-defendants, refused to turn on each other, and were showing more loyalty and stand-up toughness than many others would under the circumstances.

Three days before *AMW* ran its special about Amy's apprehension, she stood before Judge John S. McGroarty and entered a strong plea of not guilty to murder and the other charges lodged against her in the death of her late boyfriend. The woman who had looked so drawn and haggard when she was led through the terminal at McCarran Airport only a few weeks earlier, seemed to have been revitalized by her stay at the detention center. The mischievous sparkle was back in her eyes, her long hair was combed and trimmed just above her shoulders in a neat, layered look, and she had regained her sense of solid self-composure.

The defendant looked fully up to the challenge ahead of her. She didn't seem to be intimidated by the belly chains and her rumpled blue jail uniform and the shackles around her ankles and wrists as she stared the judge in the eye and emphasized the word "not" while entering her plea. Judge McGroarty, a seasoned jurist with a reputation for maintaining firm control of the proceedings in his courtroom, set a trial date for August 17 if Amy was tried separately, which attorneys for both defendants favored. October 8 was set if both Amy and Bobby were put on trial at a joint proceeding.

Defense attorneys petitioned the court to have the trials scheduled separately. "This evidence [against only one defendant] would not be admissible at a separate trial and will have a highly prejudicial spillover effect," defense lawyers wrote. As examples, the motion cited anticipated testimony linking the .380 automatic to Bobby, and the expected testimony of another witness who had seen him with a large amount of cash shortly after Bruce's death. Bobby's attorneys indicated that they would defend him by contending that he was asked to clean carpeting at his employer's home, and unwittingly agreed because he was unaware that a murder investigation would focus on the spots as possible bloodstains. Unlike his co-defendant, he did not have a financial motive, had no access to Weinstein or to his money, and no opportunity, as Amy had, to commit the murder.

Prosecutors opposed severance, claiming that the positions of the defendants were not antagonistic. Any evidence that may be admissible against one defendant could be subject to a limiting instruction from the court, and consequently severance wasn't mandatory, they asserted. Roger also pointed out that more than seventy witnesses were expected to testify, and would include people traveling from states as distant as Maine, Maryland, and Florida. Some of them would have to make the trip twice, taking them away from their families and businesses, if they were required to testify at two separate trials. The motion for severance was denied by Judge McGroarty, and he penciled in an approximate three-week period on his trial calendar beginning on October 8.

There was nothing unique about the scheduling acrobatics. Judges and attorneys keep busy professional schedules, often juggling several cases at the same time and finding dates when all the main players are available can lead to frequent conflicts. The lengthy judicial process leading up to a trial can be as slow but inexorable as clotting blood. It's the way the system works, and with Amy and Bobby slated to appear at a joint trial, scheduling problems were even more complicated than usual.

Bringing a criminal case to trial is a chess game played out by skilled legal technicians financed with taxpayer money and whatever wealth the defendants may have accumulated by legal or extra-legal means. Attorneys on each side maneuver during the pre-trial process for large and small advantages designed to give them a favorable position on the playing field when the whistle blows, or in Las Vegas terminology, the best odds. Bruce Weinstein had understood what a good player could do with an extra half-point when placing a big bet.

The defendants were spared the worry of possible conviction and execution in the death chamber at the Nevada State Prison in Carson City, where the condemned are led through an old submarine door, strapped to a gurney, and injected with a concoction of lethal drugs. Roger announced early in the proceedings that the state would not seek execution for either of the defendants. Nevada criminal codes provide the death penalty for only one capital offense, first-degree murder with aggravating circumstances. Robbery is one of those circumstances.

The Silver State doesn't send many criminals to death row, however. In slightly more than two decades after the U.S. Supreme Court's *Gregg* vs. *Georgia* decision in 1976 permitted reinstatement of the death penalty in the United States, only eight men have been executed in Nevada. At the time of the trial, only one female in the state was under sentence of death. The possibility was still left open, however, that Amy, Bobby, or both, could face life in prison.

On Thursday, October 8, 1998, more than twenty-seven months after Bruce Weinstein disappeared from his home, jury selection began at the Clark County Courthouse in downtown Las Vegas. After less than two days of examining prospective jurors, the prosecution and defense teams settled on a panel comprised of nine women and three men to determine the fate of Amy DeChant and Robert Wayne Jones. Three alternates were also selected, two women and a man.

A short time later one of the jurors provided a special Las Vegas touch to the proceedings when she was brought into the court in the absence of her fellow panelists, and apprised the judge that she had known Tony "The Ant" Spilotro. Spilotro was the notorious hoodlum who was the Chicago Mob's enforcer in Las Vegas during the 1970s and early 1980s, before he ran afoul of his bosses and was bludgeoned into unconsciousness, then buried alive with his brother, Michael, in a northwestern Indiana cornfield. The juror was permitted to remain on the jury after lawyers advised the court that they had no objection to her presence.

While tourists and local residents tossed dice, played blackjack and poker, and punched plastic buttons on thousands of slot machines just across the street in the string of posh gambling casinos that are part of the Fremont Street Experience, the prosecution and defense teams were busy inside the blocky, gray hall of justice preparing to decide the future of the man and woman accused in the Weinstein murder.

Amy's attorney Daniel Albregts was one of the stars of the Las Vegas criminal defense bar, an experienced lawyer better known for defending the type of high-profile cases that make headlines, than for everyday drug shootings, carjackings and round-ups of street floozies. Albregts represented big-money clients, who, if considered in total, tended to present an interesting buzzard's-eye view of the nasty criminal desert of Sin City. He had been the lawyer for defendants like teenager Jacob Sherwood of Sacramento, California, sentenced by a federal court judge to nineteen years in prison after he and an older companion snatched Kevin Wynn, the grown daughter of the chairman of Mirage Resorts Inc., from her home and held her for ransom. Steven Wynn paid $1.45 million, which he got from the casino cage at the Mirage, and his daughter was freed unharmed. Sherwood and Ray Cuddy were convicted on federal charges of interfering with interstate commerce through threats of violence.

Bobby Jones was represented at the trial and during pre-trial proceedings by Deputy Special Public Defenders Lee Elizabeth McMahon and Kristina Wildeveld. At the prosecution table, Roger was backed by Deputy DA Ed Kane, another experienced and hard-hitting member of Clark County District Attorney Stewart L. Bell's staff. Like Roger, Kane was a roll-up-your-sleeves, burn-the-midnight-oil type of prosecutor who believed in doing his homework and walking into the courtroom totally prepared. There were unlikely to be any surprises, no matter what the hard-working and equally determined defense teams might toss at them.

Early Monday morning, members of the panel took their seats in the jury box to listen to the opening statements of the prosecution and the defense. The shackles and jailhouse blues that the defendants had worn during pre-trial hearings had been exchanged for civilian clothes—a courtroom requirement for trials, to avoid prejudicing jurors. Bobby had shaved off his beard stubble. Amy, her layered hair perfectly styled, was modestly attired in a crisply pressed colorful print dress, with a pair of sober, sensible pumps. She had observed another birthday while behind bars, and a news reporter wrote that she looked younger than her fifty years.

Addressing the jury, Roger painted Amy as a greedy, manipulative woman, a ruthless gold digger who murdered her wealthy boyfriend after she was unable to sweet-talk him into buying property and businesses in her name. The lead prosecutor scoffed at her depiction of bookmaking as a lethally dangerous business, infested with vicious mobsters who were responsible for the savage murder of her boyfriend.

Her claim that low-life assassins with New York accents had invaded the house on the southwest edge of the city, murdered the near–300-pound gambler, then carried his body away, was a sham, he told the panel. Roger depicted Amy as a shameless, devious woman, determined to get her hands on her boyfriend's wealth one way or another. Evidence would show that the murder was about money, and that Amy had fled the state with Bruce's cash, he told the panel.

Speaking in typically measured and precise tones, Roger briefly traced Bruce's activities as an illegal bookmaker, whose bank of telephones was frequently moved from one location to another to avoid police scrutiny of his nationwide operation. "There's one salient truth in bookmaking. Fast pay makes fast friends," the prosecutor declared in a reference to the downside nature of the profession Bruce had adopted. But Roger pointed out that Bruce ran a clean family business, and didn't make enemies. He also noted that, because of Bruce's gambling activities, he was known to stash large amounts of cash under the carpets of his 4,000–square-foot house. When police searched the luxury home on Castle Vista Court, they found the corners of the carpets turned up, the Chief Deputy DA said.

Roger believes that details make the case and can spell the difference between conviction and acquittal, so he strives to be as informative as possible with juries. "It's the subtleties in the case that really drive it home to the jury," he says.

Roger also zeroed in on Amy's ominous statements about having "a plan" when she was asked why she didn't leave her boyfriend. That plan, the prosecutor declared, was to kill Bruce and, with the help of her accomplice, Bobby Jones, to dispose of the body. The prosecutor then moved to the unraveling of the scheme after Wysocki entered the picture, and the series of outrageously phony stories that Amy subsequently repeated to family members and investigators. Roger retraced the activities of the defendants as each of them twice fled the state, Bruce's body was discovered, the indictments were returned, and Amy and Bobby were ultimately brought to trial.

Amy had virtually locked herself into the defense that Albregts constructed around the basic story his client had repeatedly told to investigators and others since Bruce's disappearance. She was an innocent woman who was scared to death after killers wearing stocking masks yanked her from the shower, murdered her boyfriend, then ordered her to clean up after them and threatened to kill her if she opned her mouth. "She didn't know where to turn," the lawyer declared. "She felt like she was in a box canyon."

Albregts argued that, "if she wanted Bruce's money, it didn't make sense to kill him." After toiling for years to build a successful carpet-cleaning business and purchasing several rental properties, Amy lost everything, he told the jury. She'd had to sell out and flee to the East Coast. Referring to the state's presentation, Albregts said that the small businesswoman's only "plan" was to be financially independent.

According to the defense lawyer, Amy was "a loving significant other" who'd planned to marry the portly bookmaker, but, because she was in the house when he was killed, became the logical target for homicide investigators. He blamed Bruce's family for reputedly focusing on his client with tunnel vision, and said the evidence supported her account as much or more than the version accepted by the prosecution. Albregts said his client fled because she was afraid. "She had told police everything, and they called her a liar," the lawyer declared. "She asked for protection, and they gave her nothing."

Amy sat up straight in her chair at the defense table, listening and watching while the drama played out. Occasionally she glanced at the jury or scribbled on a yellow note pad. Bobby Jones could almost have passed for "The Invisible Man" while the prosecutor and his co-defendant's attorney dueled over her fate.

Roger identified the Las Vegas grandfather as Amy's accomplice in the scheme to relieve Bruce of a big chunk of his money, and said it was Bobby who supplied the semi-automatic that the bookie was shot with. The prosecutor also pointed out that, shortly after Bruce was murdered, Bobby cleared out of Las Vegas with a huge wad of cash. He wasn't tracked down for the second and last time until about a month after the indictments against him and his co-defendant were handed down.

Bobby's defense was basically constructed around the same arguments outlined in the earlier motion to sever the case and conduct separate trials. He'd unwittingly cleaned some stains from a carpet that were later linked to a murder investigation, and had played no knowledgeable role in the slaying. Kristina Wildeveld told the jury that her opening remarks would be shorter because her defense was clear.

"There is very little in this case to do with Robert Jones," she said.

Scavuzzo, the small-town Florida cop whose fast action led to Amy's capture in Port St. Lucie, flew into Las Vegas and spent part of one day testifying about the apprehension and related matters. After completing his testimony, he tried out some of the slot machines that Amy had recommended when he and Sergeant Thompson delivered her to the Las Vegas homicide detectives in Fort Lauderdale. She gave him bad advice.

Richard Good, the Metro police firearms expert, testified that the .380 semi-automatic found on the desert near the foot of Sunrise Mountain was the same make and caliber as the murder weapon. The prosecutor had already told the jury that the .380, which other witnesses linked to Bobby Jones, was too rusty to justify a positive conclusion that it was the weapon used to kill Bruce. Several prosecution witnesses also provided testimony about Bobby's sudden show of wealth a few days after Bruce's disappearance, describing the wad of money he showed up with, the night out at the MGM, and the defendant's purchase of an expensive new motor home.

Many of the witnesses at the trial were the same people who had testified earlier before the grand jury, and a long parade of criminalists and specialists with expertise in the forensic sciences was called to the stand. The jury was subjected to a mind-boggling array of technical testimony about the collection, preservation, and examination of crime-scene evidence, luminol, serology and DNA testing, chemical and soil analysis, identification and comparison of latent fingerprints, forensic odontology, examination of documents and handwriting identification, firearms and toolmark identification and comparisons, and causes and manner of death as determined by autopsy.

The prosecution called several active and former police officers and former employees of Bruce's to counter statements by Amy depicting the bookmaking business as inherently dangerous and infested by ruthless, kill-crazy mobsters. The prosecution witnesses testified that Bruce ran a clean, family bookmaking business that wasn't Mob-connected.

Testifying for his sister, Michael Gerber pointed out that Amy had had other long-term relationships with wealthy men that didn't result in her taking their money. Gerber and other witnesses also told the jury that she'd dated men who weren't rich.

Neither of the co-defendants chose to testify, but Amy's tape-recorded statement to Bigham and Thowsen about men identifying themselves as being with "the Mob," who invaded the luxury home to "teach Bruce a lesson," was played for the jury.

Two weeks after testimony began in the trial, the defense and the prosecution presented their closing arguments. Roger talked for more than two hours without stop. The button-down prosecutor told jurors that Bruce was shot to death after Amy failed to manipulate him into voluntarily turning his wealth over to her, so she hatched a scheme to rob him of more than $135,000 in cash and casino chips. The prosecutor suggested that she recruited her carpet-cleaning company employee as an accomplice in the robbery, and that when the scheme went awry, Bobby shot the victim with a .380-caliber pistol. "I'm not suggesting it was a planned murder," the Chief Deputy DA told the panel. "I'm suggesting . . . there was panic."

Roger scoffed at the story about tough characters who invaded the house and murdered Bruce, while claiming they didn't kill women and children and would leave her and Jaclyn alive if Amy cleaned up the bloody mess in the house. The yarn was "a sham . . . a fairy tale made up in her mind," he said. The prosecutor also told the panel that she showed a "consciousness of guilt" when she fled Las Vegas and accumulated false identification and disguises. Roger reminded the panel of Bruce's sophisticated home security system, and pointed out that he was shot in bed and there was no clothing with the body when it was found. If Amy's story was true, it would consequently mean that Bruce got out of bed and went to the door naked to let his killers inside.

Albregts delivered a scathing closing presentation that depicted the prosecution's case as being based on innuendo, rumor, and speculation. When all the evidence gathered against the defendants was added up, it was insufficient to justify convictions, he argued.

He said his client's inability to keep her stories straight about the night of the murder was a result of her terror: she was scared to death of the men who invaded her home and killed her boyfriend. Albregts reminded the jury of the testimony of some of Amy's boyfriends, who recounted her fear that she was being followed. The defense attorney told the panelists that the small fortune discovered by police when Amy was arrested in Maryland was money acquired from the sale of her property and jewelry—and that money proved she didn't need Bruce's hidden riches enough to lead her to kill him.

"They never looked at Bruce's gambling. They never looked at any other aspect of the Bruce Weinstein bookmaking business," he said. If authorities had pursued a friend of Bruce's with the same tunnel vision they focused on Amy, Albregts contended, they could have constructed an equally damaging case against a different suspect.

Evidence supported his client's story about masked intruders entering the house to "teach Bruce a lesson," murdering him, then carrying the body away, the lawyer contended. Describing his client as five-feet, one-inch tall, weighing 110 pounds, and suffering a bad hip, Albregts told the jurors that she wasn't strong enough to have lugged her boyfriend's near–300-pound body out of the house and buried it in a shallow desert grave.

Lee McMahon, one of Bobby's pauper attorneys, told the panel that her client had fled Las Vegas because he was afraid of being jailed for failing to pay child support. An appetite for the $25,000 reward posted by the Whites and Weinsteins could have inspired people close to her client to lie, she said.

Prosecutors told the jury during the rebuttal argument that the state didn't contend that Amy had moved the body. It was the prosecution's belief that Bobby Jones had handled the job of removal and burial. Kane portrayed Amy as a dominating, vindictive, greedy woman who never took no for an answer, and was determined to get Bruce's money, regardless of the cost. "Bruce Weinstein said 'no' over and over again, and now he's dead," the deputy DA declared. "The only person who ever said 'no' to Amy DeChant was Bruce Weinstein." He told the jurors, there was nothing physically she couldn't do and nothing morally she wouldn't do to get what she wanted.

The jury began deliberations on Tuesday, just over two weeks after the beginning of testimony in the exhausting proceeding, and deliberated four hours. On Thursday, after a total of fifteen hours of deliberations over three days, the panel returned its verdicts. Amy was found guilty of first-degree murder and of robbery with the use of a deadly weapon, but innocent of the charge of conspiracy to commit murder. Bobby was found guilty only of being an accessory after the fact, and innocent on the other charges. Amy looked shocked, as if she was surprised by the verdict, and her head drooped.

"The only time I think I saw her hold her head down was when she was found guilty," Bigham later recalled. "Because she thought, I mean, you know, I think she and her attorney, Albregts, thought that we weren't gonna get 'em. . . . He was definitely shocked."

The newly convicted felons each waived their right to separate penalty hearings. There would be no parade of defense witnesses talking about blighted childhoods, teenage disappointments, or youthful dedication to work with the Girl or Boy Scouts. Judge McGroarty scheduled sentencing for December 16. Amy and Bobby were handcuffed and led from the courtroom to be transported back to the detention center.

After the verdicts were announced, Sylvia White told a newspaper reporter, "All I want to do is go to the cemetery to see my son." Bruce was no longer with them, she said, but they had achieved justice.

"We had the biggest loss of our life," Bruce's white-haired father declared of his gambler son. "And now the biggest win."

Other family members began spreading the good news. As soon as Shelley Faigenblat reached the outside courthouse steps, she dialed her husband on a cell phone and told him that Amy had been convicted of Bruce's murder.

Bruce's former girlfriend was facing a term of life in prison, and the only uncertainty still left was whether or not the sentence would provide for the possibility of parole. Even if it did, the earliest Amy could become eligible for release would be after serving forty years.

Jury Foreman Cliff Moody talked with the press after the verdict, and said the panel experienced its greatest difficulty while deliberating Bobby's guilt or innocence. The jurors were unable to place him at the scene of the murder, but believed "he was responsible for cleaning up the blood." The fact that Bobby went on the run was a good indication to the jury that he was aware that a crime had occurred, the foreman said. From the beginning of the trial, the jurors had little doubt that Amy was guilty, and didn't believe the preposterous yarn about a Mob hit, Moody added.

It was later disclosed that female jurors in particular were turned off by Amy's tape-recorded dialogue with the homicide detectives. Amy seemed to be working too hard to show false emotion. The interview provided the nail that sealed her coffin. It was the story of Amy's life: She was always less convincing to women than to men.

Attorney McMahon asked the court to permit Bobby's release on $100 bail during the period between his conviction and sentencing. She argued that her client was not found guilty of murder, and was facing a sentence on a one- to six-year felony that was probational. "The man has been incarcerated for fourteen months, Judge," she said. "I think everyone learns from experience, and that includes Robert. We're asking the court to give him an opportunity to spend time with his family, to possibly contribute to their support."

Roger opposed bail, pointing to the difficulty that authorities had had running Bobby down and taking him into custody so he could be held for trial. "Judge, he's a flight risk, whether the charge is murder or pending sentencing for accessory to commit murder," the prosecutor declared. Judge McGroarty rejected the bail request, and Bobby remained behind bars.

On December 18, almost two and a half years after Bruce was shot to death in his bed, Amy, Bobby, members of their families, attorneys, and the Weinsteins assembled in the courtroom for the last time. Before sentencing, Bruce's mother was allowed to address the court. She detailed the dreadful loss that the family had experienced as a result of his murder. Bruce left behind two sisters, a brother, and a young daughter in a close-knit family who spoke with each other almost every day, she said. "There are family gatherings, and there is a chair that is always vacant." Without identifying a specific sentence she favored, Mrs. White asked the judge to give the family "peace of mind."

Roger also spoke up, noting that the state could have sought the death penalty, but didn't, and asked that Amy be sentenced to life without parole. A life sentence with the possibility of parole would send the wrong message to appellate courts or to the Pardons Board if they looked at the case some time in the future, he said. Bruce's slaying "wasn't a result of passion. It wasn't a spur-of-the-moment situation," the prosecutor declared. "This was a murder based on greed. This was a woman who loved the dollar."

Albregts did his best, but there was little for him to say except to remind the court that, even if his client was sentenced to life with the possibility of parole, Amy would be ninety years old before becoming eligible for release.

Judge McGroarty sentenced Amy to two consecutive life terms in prison without the possibility of parole. The stern jurist tacked on another twelve-year term to her life sentences for robbing the victim after shooting him, and ordered it also to be served consecutively. The sentence included stipulations ordering her to pay $5,000 in restitution, $2,749.64 in extradition costs, and submit to genetic testing at her own expense of $250. Bobby was also ordered to submit to genetic testing and pay the $250.

Dressed once again in jailhouse blues, in handcuffs, shackles, and belly chains, Amy stood quietly beside her lawyer, facing the judge with the corners of her mouth turned slightly down while the sentence was pronounced. Heeding the advice of her attorney, she chose not to address the court.

The grasping, deceitful woman, who'd told boyfriends that she wanted to retire by the time she was fifty, would be spending the rest of her life in an austere, repressive environment where she would be fed, clothed, and provided with medical care. She was permanently out of the rat race and would never again need to worry about building up a comfortable nest egg for retirement. The *SUN* quoted Bruce's family as saying that they preferred the life sentence over the death penalty because Bruce's killer would have to "live in a cage for at least 40 years" before she was free again.

Before McGroarty pronounced sentence on Amy's crony, Bobby pleaded for leniency, advising the judge that he had several job offers and wanted to be free so he could work and support his family. McMahon also asked the judge to order probation for her client, observing that he was essentially convicted of cleaning a carpet. Several letters had been mailed earlier by family members, including grandchildren of the convicted man, pleading with the jurist not to order Bobby to serve additional time behind bars.

Moments later, while members of the fifty-nine-year-old poker-playing grandfather's family sat in the spectator seats sobbing, McGroarty sentenced him to serve at least two years in prison. Bobby was given credit for the fourteen months already spent in the Clark County Detention Center.

Dressed in baggy prison blues and shackled hand and foot, the convicts were returned to their cells at the detention center to await transportation to Nevada state prisons.

AFTERWORD

Amy Rica DeChant is serving her life sentence at a private Nevada state prison for women in the municipality of North Las Vegas, just a few minutes' drive from her former home at the Castle Vista Estates.

The sparkling new 500-bed Southern Nevada Women's Correctional Facility, with dormitories and pods accommodating inmates on different security levels ranging from trustee to maximum, was opened for business in December 1997, just two months after the indictments were returned.

The first inmates began arriving three days after the final inspection was completed, and two weeks later 400 women from all over the state were already locked up there. Most of the women were bused from an overcrowded 260-bed women's prison in Carson City. The old prison was converted for use by male inmates and renamed the Warm Springs Correctional Center.

Construction and operation of the new forty-three-acre, $25-million women's penitentiary by the Nashville, Tennessee–based Corrections Corporation of America (CCA) is an experiment, and marked the first time that a private business was granted authority to operate a prison in the Silver State. The agreement between the Nevada Department of Prisons and CCA provides a way out for the state if authorities are dissatisfied with the way the institution is operated. Nevada can simply pay the corporation for the cost of construction, take over, and operate it themselves. But that isn't likely to happen.

Some observers credit private prisons run by CCA, its largest competitor, the Wackenhut Corrections Corporation, and other companies in the rapidly expanding business, with running a cleaner, more secure operation that has fewer problems than the old system. Privately run prisons can also cost the taxpayers less than state-operated institutions. When Amy was processed into the North Las Vegas facility, Nevada was paying CCA $40 per day to house and control each inmate. The daily per-inmate cost at the Carson City facility was almost $5 more per day.

As far as the inmates are concerned, daily life in the CCA-operated multi-custody penitentiary is about the same as it would be in any other prison. At the lockup, Amy and most of her fellow inmates are awakened at 7 a.m. in their alphabetically organized dormitories, and, while guards go down the list calling out letters, the women report to the commissary for breakfast.

At 8 a.m., they report to work stations or school, attend therapy sessions, or participate in other organized activities such as Alcoholics and Narcotics Anonymous meetings, classes in parenting and anger management, and—for inmates about to be released—a course of instruction called "street readiness."

Teachers from the Clark County School District drive to the prison to instruct high school classes, and the first graduation ceremony occurred in June, about four months before Amy went on trial. Jobs include work in the laundry room, beauty shop, and other in-house operations that support and service the inmate population. Time is shaved off the prison terms of most inmates who choose jobs or school attendance, but Amy is not one of those women with an opportunity to work for early release, because of the "no parole" stipulation in her sentence.

Most inmates who aren't working, in the classroom, or busy with some other organized activity, and haven't broken the rules and lost privileges, are allowed to mix with each other in dayrooms or participate in other activities. They can lounge on plastic outdoor furniture, watch soap operas on television, work with arts and crafts, play softball, or work out in a weight room. According to corrections spokesmen, the weight room at the women's penitentiary is the least popular activity, which is just the opposite of the situation at men's prisons.

Despite the amenities, the institution is every bit a prison, and guards stationed inside locked towers at every corridor intersection closely monitor the movements of each inmate. Outside, the monolithic, block-style facility is surrounded by razor wire. There can be no mistaking what the grim institution on Smiley Road is there for.

Amy DeChant isn't the only convicted murderess or even the most notorious killer among the women she shares her home with. The dubious title as the institution's most infamous inmate belongs to an evil-tempered seventy-year-old black woman, Priscilla Ford, who is the only female out of eighty-four people under sentence of death in Nevada. Ford drove her Lincoln Continental onto a crowded sidewalk in Reno on Thanksgiving Day 1980, then deliberately steered it through dozens of screaming pedestrians at high speed. When the vehicle finally came to a stop, six people were dead or dying and another twenty-one were injured.

It's unlikely that Amy and the woman who carried out Nevada's so-called "Thanksgiving Day Massacre" will ever see each other. Amy's status as a convicted murderess doesn't mean she will be locked up in a cell by herself for twenty-three hours a day like Priscilla Ford. Women serving sentences for homicide may share most of the privileges of their fellow inmates who are doing time for lesser offenses. The quality of an inmate's behavior inside counts for a lot, and according to a Nevada Department of Prisons spokesman, administrators prefer not to deprive women of freedoms that it isn't necessary to withhold.

The grandfather whom Amy dragged with her into the tragedy surrounding Bruce's murder was also assigned to a prison only a few minutes' drive from his home in Las Vegas. Bobby Jones served the remaining months of his sentence at the Southern Desert Correctional Center (SDCC) in the dusty little town of Indian Springs. The SDCC is an old-fashioned Nevada prison, located just off U.S. Highway 95 about forty miles north of Las Vegas.

David J. J. Roger, the Chief Deputy District Attorney who headed the prosecution team, was busy early in 1999 working on a challenging new case surrounding the reputed murder of a member of one of Las Vegas's gambling royal families. Ted Binion, a wealthy playboy, heir to the $30 million casino fortune linked to Binion's Horseshoe, where the best card players in the world gather for the annual World Series of Poker, died of an overdose of heroin and the prescription sedative Xanax in September. A few weeks later police arrested his former topless dancer girlfriend and others and charged them with engineering the playboy junkie's death. The case is still in the courts.

Ed Kane, who was second chair during the twin trial of

Amy and Bobby, prosecuted a case and won a sentence of four life prison terms without the possibility of parole against a man who murdered his girlfriend and another man he believed was her lover when he saw them climb into a car together. After the slaying, the killer learned that the man he shot was merely giving the young woman a ride—and that the driver's wife and child were also in the car. In another case still making its way through the courts, Kane was also prosecuting a sixteen-year-old boy accused of fatally shooting through a door and killing a man during a dispute over loud music.

Kristina Wildeveld, one of the Deputy Special Public Defenders who represented Bobby Jones, also continued to keep busy, and one of her clients was accused in a reputed murder-for-hire scheme connected to a member of the wealthy du Pont family. Wildeveld and Kane, who were on opposite sides in the Weinstein murder trial, again squared off against each other in a case involving the fatal shooting of a sixteen-year-old girl in a teenage love triangle. In a plea-bargain deal, the killer, also sixteen at the time of the shooting, pleaded guilty to second-degree murder with use of a deadly weapon, and was sentenced to a long prison term.

Amy's lawyer, Daniel Albregts, continued to make local headlines with his representation of clients in notorious murder cases, including a defendant in the Mob hit of a longtime Las Vegas hoodlum tied to organized crime, "Fat Herbie" Blitzstein. Fat Herbie was a real-life version of the ruthless organized crime assassins on whom Amy blamed her boyfriend's murder, and was shot down in his home by a couple of hitmen. When "Tony the Ant" Spilotro was a Las Vegas Mob kingpin, Blitzstein was known as a brutal enforcer and Spilotro's right-hand man. At the time of Blitzstein's death, organized crime families from California and Buffalo, New York, were reportedly putting the pressure on to take over his loan-sharking business.

Albregts's client, Antone Davi, pleaded guilty as part of a plea bargain agreement in U.S. District Court in Las Vegas to being one of the two hitmen who carried out the contract in a scheme that ultimately involved more than one dozen defendants. Davi, who agreed to testify against codefendants as part of the pact, was scheduled for sentencing after their trials.

Blitzstein was a longtime friend of Ted Binion and when the casino mogul's gaming license was revoked and he was forced to give up his twenty-percent interest in the Horseshoe several months before his death, authorities cited his close ties with members of organized crime as part of the reason for the action. A few weeks before his murder, Blitzstein was nominated by state gaming agents for Nevada's infamous "Black Book" of undesirables who are barred from casinos. In Las Vegas, gangsters, gamers, and politicians often grieve at the same funerals.

By early 1999 Judge McGroarty had applied his talents and legal acumen to a variety of felony trials ranging from murder to the plea-bargained sentencing of a balding forty-three-year-old glamour photographer who romanced a twelve-year-old would-be model and planned to run off to Italy and marry her when she turned sixteen. The girl insisted that she was in love with the photographer and refused to cooperate with prosecutors, so the lensman was permitted to plead to scaled-down charges and was sentenced to two to five years in prison with lifetime parole.

McGroarty also traveled to Lovelock in northwestern Nevada to preside over a competency hearing for one of the most notorious serial murderers in the histories of California and the Silver State. The hearing at the courthouse in Pershing County was scheduled after a federal appeals court threw out the death sentence of Gerald Gallego, claiming that the judge in the case erred when he suggested to a jury that the sex-slave killer might eventually win parole if he wasn't executed. Gallego, who murdered two teenage girls kidnapped from a Sacramento shopping mall after driving them to Nevada, was also sentenced to death in California for slayings there. After a three-day competency trial, Judge McGroarty ruled that the killer was mentally fit to participate in a retrial of the Nevada death penalty proceedings.

Mike Wysocki was busy doing what he does so well, peering into the shadows and snooping into other people's lives—and deaths. Amy didn't telephone him anymore, and the last time he heard from her was a couple of days before he appeared on one of the *America's Most Wanted* broadcasts in March 1997. Wysocki figured that the phone calls would stop after she saw his interview on the show, and his instincts were on target.

Detective Thomas Thowsen was also working on the Binion case with a new partner, Detective Jim Buczek. Buczek was lead investigator. In addition, Thowsen was working on a case focusing on a father, his two sons, and two nephews accused of tracking and shooting up a pickup truck and killing two of the three occupants.

On June 3, 1999, Bigham was next up on the Homicide Divison detective rotation when a young part-time nightclub bouncer recently released from the Marines stomped into an Albertsons supermarket two miles east of the Strip a few minutes before dawn and began blasting away at employees. When the shooting stopped, three men and a woman were dead or dying, and another young man was seriously wounded. Twenty-three-year-old Zane Michael Floyd, wearing a goatee, dressed in military camouflage, his head shaven, was arrested at the scene with a pump-action shotgun. He was jailed on four counts of murder and a single charge of attempted murder. Additional charges were filed against Floyd after a twenty-year-old woman working for Love Bound, an outcall escort service, reported that she was sent to his house where he handcuffed, raped, and sodomized her shortly before setting off on the killing rampage. The woman, who had arrived in town from Portland, Oregon, only a few months earlier, said Floyd told her that he was trained to kill, had nineteen shotgun shells, and was going to kill the first nineteen people he saw.

District Attorney Bell decided to prosecute the case personally because he was anticipating a psychological defense strategy, and he had special expertise in the field. Bell, who had formerly worked as a mental commitment judge, said he would ask for the death sentence.

Police, prosecutors, judges, and other officers of the court are locked in a grim, never-ending frontline battle to punish the guilty and protect the innocent. They are soldiers in the constant fire-fights that flare and explode in the city's violent criminal subculture. It is all part of the morbid pastiche that is life and death in Las Vegas!

While destroying Bruce Weinstein, Amy inflicted a lifetime of trauma and loss on his family. Life will never be the same for the Whites and the Weinsteins, but they've earned a modicum of peace knowing that they helped bring the woman responsible for Bruce's death to justice and that she will never again troll the poker tables at the Mirage, the Orleans, or any other casino for rich men who could afford her. Sylvia White played an especially seminal role in bringing her son's killer to justice, and was one of the first to recognize Amy for the coldly calculating, predatory gold digger that she was.

Before Amy and her crony were put on trial, Fred and Sylvia White became actively involved with the local Families of Murder Victims support group, after being told about the organization by a friend. The FMV is part of a grass-roots national movement encompassing various organizations serving the growing number of families of the victims of murder and other forms of violence who have abandoned the old concept of suffering in silence. The same thing that Mothers Against Drunk Driving (MADD) did in the 1970s, victims' rights advocates are doing in the courtroom, in the legislatures, and in the streets today: fighting to make the justice system work for victims. For survivors like the Whites and others who have lost loved ones to violence, fighting back can serve as a catharsis and help them regain control of their lives.

Banding together, groups like Families of Murder Victims have pushed for new laws to force the courts to recognize the people left behind when violence strikes. They sponsor fund-raising activities and demonstrate at protest appearances; members sit beside grieving parents, spouses, children, and siblings to provide support and comfort during emotionally agonizing trials.

Fighting back is part of a national trend by victims and family members, as advocates demand important changes in the justice system. Members of the loose coalition of advocates' groups have either achieved or are still pushing for demands that survivors be notified of trial dates, be allowed to attend trials, comment on plea agreements and discuss cases with prosecutors, be notified of the release of violators and comment on parole, be paid compensation, and be permitted to present impact statements. Not every group supports every goal, but working separately and together the victims' organizations have become a potent political force.

Mrs. White was able to address the court minutes before the sentencing of her son's killer because Nevada and at least twenty-seven other states now permit family members to give victims' impact statements following convictions. Several states also permit family members to witness executions of convicted killers.

Winning the right to present impact statements wasn't easy, and the U.S. Supreme Court twice ruled against it in 1987 and in 1989, rejecting the evidence as inflammatory. Then a more conservative court bolstered with appointments by Republican President George Bush overturned the previous rulings in a 6-to-3 decision in 1991, determining that the Eighth Amendment does not bar a jury from considering evidence dealing with a victim's survivors.

Some cities now have victims' outreach centers that provide comprehensive services including legal advice, individual and group counseling and other help to crime victims and their survivors. Many police departments have victims' services divisions and specialists, and some courthouses have victims' respite rooms where people can go to grieve, or to get themselves together after too much emotional battering. District Attorney Bell maintains a Victim Witness Assistance Center in his office spaces at the Clark County Courthouse.

While Amy and Bobby Jones were on trial in Las Vegas, 2,000 miles east in New York, a new computer tracking system called the Victim Information & Notification Everyday (VINE) began operating. VINE operates a twenty-four-hour hotline for registered crime victims, so they can keep track of an inmate's status and whereabouts in the justice system. Crime victims can also arrange to receive computerized telephone calls notifying them minutes after an offender posts bond, is released from custody, or escapes.

While Amy DeChant grows old in prison, many of the people whose lives she crossed and so greatly altered or affected will continue to ponder why she embarked on the particular path she chose and committed so many hurtful acts. With only a few exceptions, she heaped her worst abuse on the people who loved her most. That was certainly the case with Bruce Weinstein, who took her into his heart, his home, and his bed, and was repaid for his affection and generosity in the most savage manner possible.

She was a septic "Typhoid Mary," who infected the people around her with touches of her contagion. Friends, business associates, and sweethearts who wandered too close to her either found themselves in serious trouble with the law, explaining embarrassing involvements to investigators, reeling with broken hearts—or dead. Many of the beaus Amy dragged into her troubles were average, middle-aged, working-class men who were never in trouble with the law over anything more serious than parking tickets. They were hurt, frightened, and embarrassed, and when homicide detectives contacted them for interviews, often stuttered, hyperventilated, and gasped for air. They were scared to death.

Amy's loyal brother, Michael "Mickey" Gerber, also suffered because of her runaway greed. He was subpoenaed as a witness and dragged through the misery and embarrassment of seeing his beloved sister prosecuted and convicted for the murder of her boyfriend.

Bobby Jones may not be the type of person many people would seek out as a neighbor, but he seemed to be staying out of serious trouble and was a loving, attentive grandfather doing his best to care for his family . . . until he fell under the noxiously destructive influence of his boss.

When detectives talked with John Gerard in New Brunswick, he told them that his friend George Sackel still didn't believe the terrible things that were being said about Amy. If Gerard had been so damaged by his experiences in Vietnam and been the kind of man Amy apparently thought he was, he could have been doing time in prison instead of Bobby Jones. But the New Jersey property manager was disgusted by her horrific suggestion that he fly to Ohio and kill a man for her so that she could gain control of his wealth. Although Gerard had enjoyed her company and their friendship went back several years, he never talked to her again.

Amy also betrayed a string of other men who loved or otherwise had deep affection for her, including some who put their own reputations, finances, freedom, and safety at risk by standing by her during difficult and perilous times. She rejected the love of some of her beaus because they couldn't afford her, and others, apparently, because it was simply inconvenient. A man she lived with in Florida told Bigham that she would be welcome in a heartbeat if she came back to him. Joe Kosa must have agonized as he sat at his kitchen table watching the woman who had shared his home being handcuffed and taken away by police to face charges of murder. Interviewed weeks after Amy's arrest at her home, Kosa told *AMW* that he hadn't noticed "a mean streak in her body." They had a wonderful time together, he said.

Amy killed the one man who could afford her, because he wouldn't sign over a big chunk of his riches to finance business ventures or home-buying schemes she hatched. It was a terrible waste of Bruce Weinstein's life.

But ultimately, Amy wasted her own life, frittering away her opportunities for happiness in a non-stop orgy of greed and an apparently overwhelming desire to validate her own self-worth by enticing, manipulating, and emotionally abusing or robbing a series of men. During all or most of her adult life she played the sex card while misusing one man after another, and didn't hesitate to entangle an occasional woman friend to further her labyrinthian schemes, or simply to make things a bit easier.

She tried her charms out on the men she worked with, she tried them on Mike Wysocki, on Sheriff's Sergeant Douglas Verzi, and on Paul Bigham and Tom Thowsen when she posed as the poor little girl whom everyone was picking on, and interrupted her question-and-answer session to ask for a hug. "Amy," Wysocki observed to the grand jurors, "likes to control men."

If Amy had truly hungered for love and affection, it was there for the taking. Time and again she proved her ability to attract the admiration, love, and devotion of men. She could have settled down with one of them in a warm and rewarding relationship, but she was too driven by the inner demons inside her mind. She ruthlessly squandered the opportunities, and tossed them away.

Amy DeChant didn't have to waste her adult life dealing from the bottom of the deck to the people who trusted her most. She was an energetic, intelligent, attractive woman who had other options, and proved she could be successful in legitimate enterprise. But she preferred the challenge and pleasure of seducing, then betraying, men.

Despite all her ready intelligence, Amy wasn't really all that cunning, and she made some terrible mistakes, beginning with Bruce's murder and throughout the investigation. Her performance in Harford County, Maryland, was abysmal, and it seemed that, beginning with the heavy foot that led to her being stopped for speeding, she did almost everything wrong. She had the cold heart of a Barbary Coast pirate, but she lacked much in criminal expertise, and it led to her downfall.

As Detective Bigham observed during an appearance on *America's Most Wanted*: "Strange individual. She was cutting firewood in the nude with a chain saw . . . It's dangerous too, I think."

Amy Dechant is all that and more, strange and dangerous; a woman of intrigue and mystery.

Amy studied and learned from her lovers, and the homicide detectives who helped put an end to her speckled career as an alluring *femme fatale* are still wondering if she may have tried a little bookmaking on her own. For a while she owned a house in an older part of the city with several telephone lines leading inside. There were too many telephones for a normal residence, but enough to support a bookmaking operation. After years of peering into her life, there is still much that police and other investigators don't know about Amy DeChant.

UPDATE 2004

Amy DeChant may have been a lot of things in her life, a ruthless schemer, a malignantly seductive Lorelei, and a killer—but one thing she is not, is a quitter. And early in the new millennium her stubborn persistence in attempting to win her eventual freedom paid off.

Two years after she was ordered to spend the rest of her life behind bars, she beat the odds by opening up an opportunity to walk out of prison a free woman before the end of the decade.

The Nevada State Supreme Court dealt the imprisoned murderess a winning hand in October 2000 by ruling that major errors were made in her trial. The court threw out her first-degree murder conviction and ordered a new proceeding.

During arguments in a Las Vegas courtroom, Amy's appeal lawyer Daniel Albregts, argued that prosecutors presented insufficient evidence and that the trial judge committed several errors. Albregts declared that his client was "a woman who was convicted of a murder she did not commit."

The attorney struck especially hard at Al Leavitt's remarks before the jury, describing Amy's story blaming mobsters for her boyfriend's murder as a "fairy tale" that he didn't believe, even though Judge McGroarty had ordered the witness to steer away from voicing his personal opinions. McGroarty instructed the jury to disregard Leavitt's skeptical remarks, but even after the crusty retired detective left the witness stand they were brought up again in the prosecution's closing arguments.

"Given the crucial nature of Leavitt's testimony and the prosecutors' paraphrasing of Leavitt's opinion during closing, we cannot say that the error was harmless," the three-judge panel wrote in a unanimous opinion.

The panel also ruled that Judge McGroarty should have required Wysocki to share the notes he gathered during his investigation with the defense.

The possibility of a rematch with Amy's old courtroom nemesis David J. J. Roger was avoided when the new trial was assigned to another veteran prosecutor, Chief Deputy District Attorney Edward Kane. Roger was busy with the Binion case and other prosecutions, before eventually winning election in 2002 as Clark County District Attorney and replacing his former boss.

Months before Roger's successful foray into local politics, Amy sidestepped the ordeal of an emotionally exhausting retrial by accepting a plea bargain that called for her to plead guilty to second-degree murder.

Provisions of the guilty plea required her to admit only that the prosecution could prove its case against her, and during the plea and sentencing proceeding she pounced on the opportunity to demonstrate some of her old audaciousness.

Addressing members of her victim's family, Amy remarked, "We both feel a tremendous loss due to Bruce's death."

And after thanking the judge and the prosecutor for their fair play and willingness to compromise, she declared:

"Although the mystery has not been solved, I am accepting this agreement so everyone involved can hopefully find peace and go on with their lives."

Judge McGroarty ordered a new 25-year sentence with the possibility of parole after serving ten years. With credit for the more than three years she had already served, the new sentence opened up the chance that she could be released well before the end of the decade.